sewing
made simple

threads

sewing
made simple

The Essential
Guide to Teaching
Yourself to Sew

Editors of Threads

The Taunton Press
Inspiration for hands-on living®

The Taunton Press, Inc.,
63 South Main Street,
PO Box 5506,
Newtown, CT 06470-5506
e-mail: tp@taunton.com

Editors: Sarah Rutledge Gorman and Renee Iwaszkiewicz Neiger
Copy editor: Candace B. Levy
Indexer: Cathy Goddard
Cover and interior design: Laura Palese
Layout: Susan Lampe Wilson
Illustrators: Casey Lukatz and Christine Erikson

Threads® is a trademark of The Taunton Press, Inc.,
registered in the U.S. Patent and Trademark Office.

The following names/manufacturers appearing in
Threads Sewing Made Simple are trademarks:
Dacron®, Dupioni®, Ethafoam®, Lycra®, Microtex®,
Polarfleece®, Tencel®, Ultrasuede®

Library of Congress Cataloging-in-Publication Data

Threads sewing made simple : the essential guide to
teaching yourself to sew / Editors of Threads.
     pages cm
  Includes index.
  ISBN 978-1-60085-956-4
1. Sewing--Handbooks, manuals, etc. I. Threads magazine.
II. Title: Sewing made simple.
  TT705.T495 2013
  646'.19--dc23
                            2013013866

Printed in the United States of America
10 9 8 7 6 5 4 3 2 1

dedication

For people who love to sew

acknowledgments

Thanks to Sarah Rutledge Gorman for combing through the *Threads* archive and selecting information that is most helpful to those learning to sew. She skillfully organized it with the help of her editor, Renee Neiger. Thanks to the Taunton Press book staff and everyone who worked so hard to make this book look as good as it does.

Special thanks to all of our *Threads* authors, contributors, and editors. Without you, this book would not have been possible.

contents

introduction

So you want to learn to sew. Good for you! Making your own clothing, bags, pillows, and more is a great way to express your creativity. Whether you're brand new to the craft or have a handle on the basics but want to learn more, we're here to help.

Starting in the early 20th century, sewing was included in school and college curricula because it was perceived as a money-saving skill that women needed to run a household smoothly. By the mid-1980s, this was no longer true. Ready-to-wear clothing had become less expensive, and the rapid expansion of discount stores made it easier for women in all areas to find affordable attire. Women were also working outside the home in greater and greater numbers. Many had no time to spare for sewing, while others viewed it as an outdated form of drudgery. At the same time, schools began phasing out home economics classes and investing more money in technology. Where it was once common for students to learn the basics of sewing, today many young people have never had a lesson.

Things have changed. Women—and men!—are embracing the art of sewing. If you value good quality and great fit, if you want to avoid overconsumption of goods, and if you enjoy the idea of wearing the fruits of your self-expression, sewing is for you. Technology has made today's sewing machines incredibly user friendly, and most models are chock-full of handy gadgets to help you (see p. 22 for more). Anything else you design is a static object, but sewing produces a moving, fluid creation that celebrates the shape of the human body. When you begin to understand elements of color, texture, shape, and line, incredibly personal creations will emerge.

The book is organized into four parts. First, we take you through getting started, and then we offer nine pattern-free projects for you to try. After that, we walk you through understanding patterns and basic garment layout, followed by nine more projects with patterns included. We explain sewing terms as we go, but if you can't remember the difference between an armscye (armhole) and weft (crosswise threads), you can always turn to the Glossary on p. 156. Now let's get started!

getting started

We know, we know: You've been itching to learn how to sew for weeks, months, maybe even years—and now that you've got this book in hand, you're ready to jump into that delicious world of color and texture and model your new creation later tonight. Don't worry, you'll get there! But first we have to get you set up.

- - - - - - - - - - - - - - - - - - - ✿ - - - - - - - - - - - - - - - - - - -

You're going to need a place to work, whether it's a corner of your studio apartment, an extra room in your house, or a portable setup you take along with you or slide in and out of sight. Once you're situated, you'll have fun shopping for tools and supplies, including the big kahuna—your very own sewing machine. We'll run through the basic hand and machine stitches you need to throw together everything from a simple scarf to a form-fitting wrap dress, and we'll give you the lowdown on finishing and pressing. (We can't have you out on the town with raggedy edges!) And while you're gearing up for garment greatness, it doesn't hurt to have a few practical skills at hand, like mending torn clothing, replacing a button, and changing around your hems for a better fit.

Once you're ready to roll, you can either turn right to our pattern-free projects in Chapter 2, or learn about patterns and what's involved with them in Chapter 3. Either way, you're going to have to make some room in your closet for all your beautiful new creations.

setting up your sewing space

Before you start sewing, you may want to establish a place to create your alluring attire. If you have the space for a dedicated sewing room, go for it! But sewing doesn't require its own room. In fact, many a lovely summer dress has been made at the kitchen table. Work with what you have.

Getting organized

You can find the cutting, sewing, and storage space you need to sew even if you have a small apartment. The following tips also work if you're looking for portable or foldaway solutions.

SEWING TABLE When setting up your sewing table, movement is key. You can put a sewing machine on almost any table—kitchen, card, dining, or picnic—but a rolling one is best. You can leave your machine set up, but you'll have the flexibility to move it out of the way when you're not using it. An old, inexpensive computer table makes a perfect sewing machine workstation; the keyboard shelf is just the right size and height. And a desk-height rolling drawer unit is great for storing scissors, thread, machine attachments, and notions. If possible, set up your table near a full-length mirror, or add one to the space. You don't want to walk around every time you have to check a garment's fit.

If you have the room, create a dedicated sewing space.

CHAIR AND LIGHTING The chair that holds your body for hours of sewing is your most important piece of sewing room furniture. The key is adjustability: Look for a chair that allows you to make modifications to fit your shape. Adjust your seat height until your knees are bent at 90 degrees to 110 degrees. There should be no pressure on the back of your legs. The height of your sewing surface should keep your elbows at right angles, forearms parallel to the floor. To prevent eyestrain, use task lighting (such as an adjustable desk lamp) at your work area, even if you have a good source of natural light or a strong overhead.

make it simple

Limited sewing space means you need to make good use of every inch, so a handy way to store buttons, snaps, and other small items is in a revolving spice rack. The multiple jars fit neatly into the rack, and you can see what you're looking for with one quick spin. Place a pin holder right on top for easy access.

If needed, you can share your sewing space with another room.

Portable or foldaway solutions allow you to take your sewing with you wherever you go.

CUTTING TABLE You can put a dining table, pool table, and empty kitchen counter into service for a quick cutting project. But if you don't have one of these and you need to create a sturdy cutting surface, place ½-inch-thick foamcore sheets (available at art-supply stores) on your bed, then slide your cutting mat on top to lay out and cut your pattern. You can also place an ironing board next to a small table, and adjust the board's height to create a temporary, continuous cutting surface.

STORAGE Some under-the-bed boxes have wheels. You can roll them around the room when you need them, and hide them when you don't. Smaller supplies fit easily into baskets and designer boxes. If you want to see your fabric stash at a glance, secure each piece of fabric to a skirt hanger, and place the hangers on a closet rod sorted by colors. If you don't have the space, try storing fabric and patterns in your luggage. Another solution, for a larger space, is to piggyback two inexpensive, backless bookshelves, one in front of the other. These extra-deep shelves can accommodate bolts of fabric, just like at a fabric store.

STORYBOARD No matter what size space you have, a storyboard gives you an overview of your ideas that you won't see any other way. It's a great method for gathering and displaying your inspirations, a place to collect your thoughts and arrange information about your collection. Hang or lean a large corkboard at eye level, and post fabric swatches, fashion illustrations, fashion show photos, paint color chips, flowers, sketches, cut-out letters and words, notes, shapes, your own photos, fabric and sewing swatches, thread and yarn, color combinations, outfit possibilities, buttons, and more. Add anything that inspires you. As the storyboard develops a vibe and direction, your personality begins to show through it. The assembled colors, shapes, and ideas contribute to making your creations unique.

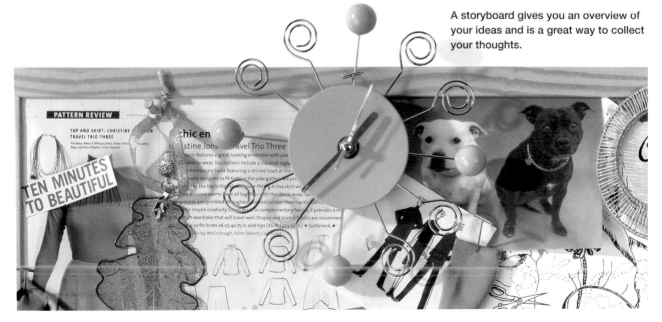

A storyboard gives you an overview of your ideas and is a great way to collect your thoughts.

tools and supplies

An important part of sewing is having the right tools. For ease and accuracy, you need tools for measuring, marking, cutting, securing, sewing, and embellishing. Many of the basic sewing tools are so simple and so well designed, they've remained essentially unchanged for centuries.

- -

Measuring

With the following precision aids in hand, you can get all the measurements you need, check for accuracy as you sew, and even alter patterns for a better fit.

RULER Use a ruler to draft patterns or measure fabric; a transparent one is handy because you can see the material underneath. Some models have slots at regular intervals so you can mark right though the ruler.

See-Thru Ruler

Dritz

MEASURING TAPE A tape measure is an indispensable tool for taking body measurements. Those made from cloth tend to stretch, fray, or tear over time, so you're better off with one made from plastic or reinforced fiberglass and with reinforced metal tips. Check it against a hard ruler occasionally to ensure accuracy.

To be a successful sewer, you must have the right tools—and know how to use them.

SEAM GAUGE A seam gauge allows you to measure hems, seam allowances, tucks, pleats, and buttons. A slider holds the measurement until you reposition it.

FRENCH CURVE The perimeter and interior cutouts of clear plastic drafting templates, called French curves, feature a variety of curves, which can be used in part or whole to draw graceful necklines, collars, and armscyes (armholes) on an original design or to true a pattern you are altering.

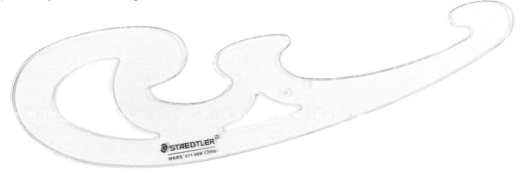

Marking

When you start using patterns, you'll need to transfer the marks from the pattern to your fabric so you'll know exactly where important landmarks occur, such as the dart point, the zipper base, and the buttonhole position.

MARKING WHEELS Marking wheels come with different edges, and each edge type has a specific purpose. Notched or smooth tracing wheels are used with dressmaker's tracing paper to transfer marks from patterns to the fabric's wrong side before sewing. A pinpoint tracing wheel punches a trail through and under any line it follows, making it ideal for transferring a pattern onto paper.

CHALK Chalk markers aren't 100 percent chalk; they usually include wax or clay. You can find chalk in solid and powder varieties. What the markers are made of determines how easily they can be removed from the fabric. Powdered chalk enables you to draw precise but temporary lines on fabric. Many professionals use tailor's chalk to mark clothes for alteration or record seamlines and match points on muslins. Clay chalk is usually used on thinner or delicate fabrics because you can brush it away. You can purchase a plastic holder and sharpener that makes this chalk more efficient to use. Wax chalk leaves marks that disappear when touched with a hot iron and is most often used on thick fabrics that readily absorb the mark as it melts.

Pinpoint
tracing wheel

Smooth
tracing wheel

Notched
tracing wheel

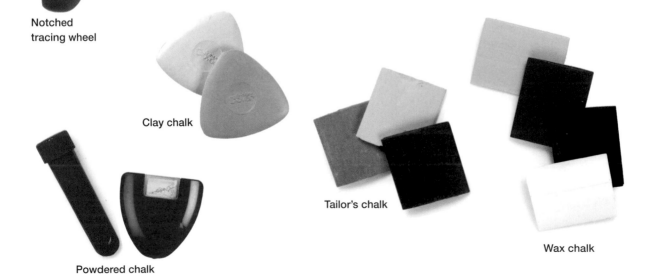

Clay chalk

Tailor's chalk

Powdered chalk

Wax chalk

Pens and pencils

Felt-tipped pens and mechanical pencils make fine removable marks. (You can use a number of methods to remove the marks.)

DISAPPEARING MARKING PENS Disappearing pens come in two varieties. One makes marks that disappear as the ink dries over a few days, and the other makes marks that disappear with a spritz or daub of water. Both are handy, but always test them on your fabric before using. Make sure to remove these marks before using an iron, or they might become permanent.

FABRIC MARKING PENCILS You can find fabric marking pencils in traditional wood or mechanical versions. They have a variety of colored leads, some chalk-based, and deliver a fine, erasable mark.

Chalk pencil

Disappearing-ink pen

Cutting

A good pair of scissors is important in garment sewing, but one pair often just doesn't seem to be enough. There are plenty of sewing scissors available, including many specialty models designed for every task. Some are essential equipment, whereas others are just nice to have, depending on your needs.

SHEARS All cutting instruments with two crossing blades are called *scissors*, but shears have a large finger ring and a small one for the thumb and are usually longer than 6 inches. Shears (sometimes referred to as trimmers) are meant for all-purpose cutting, and they can be straight or bent; the bent variety is designed for cutting on a flat surface. Bent-handle versions should help keep the fabric flat while cutting, and spring-loaded, straight versions should reduce hand fatigue.

Microserrated shears are used for knits and silky fabrics. Small scissors (often called embroidery or craft scissors) are for clipping, trimming, and detail cutting. All scissors should have sharp blades and points and be comfortable to hold and easy to handle. Nippers, also known as thread clippers, snip threads while sewing and clip through multiple layers easily. Pinking shears create a neat zigzag edge that discourages raveling. Use your favorite scissors on fabric only. To further prolong the life and sharpness of your scissors, use a soft cloth to wipe off the inside of each blade after use to eliminate fiber debris or moisture that may cling to the blades.

Knife-edge straight trimmers, 8 inches

Bent shears, 8 inches

Easy-action, spring-assist shears

Microserrated shears, 8¼ inches

Spring-action embroidery scissors, 4 inches

Needlecraft scissors, 4 inches

Stork embroidery scissors, 3½ inches

Nippers

Pinking shears

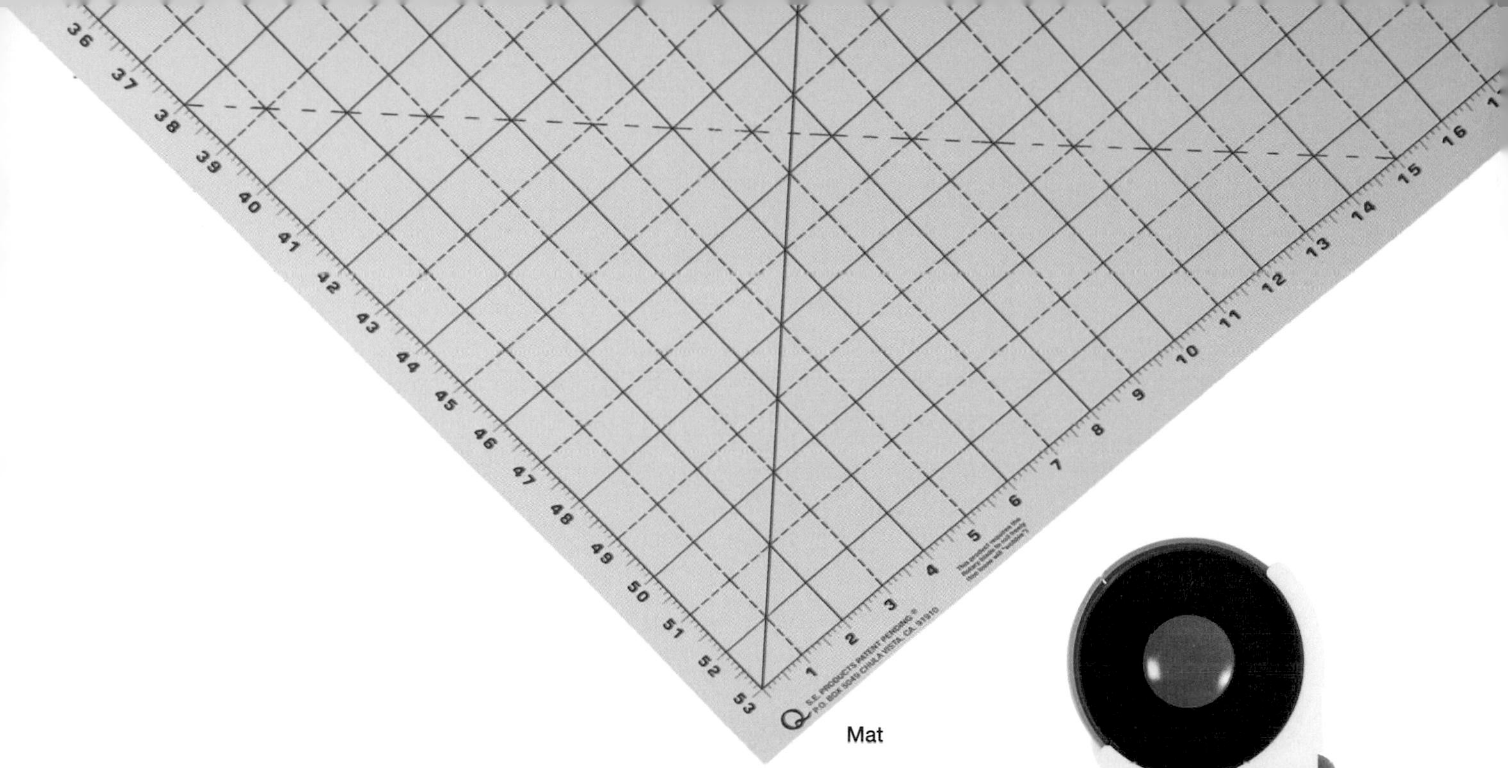

Mat

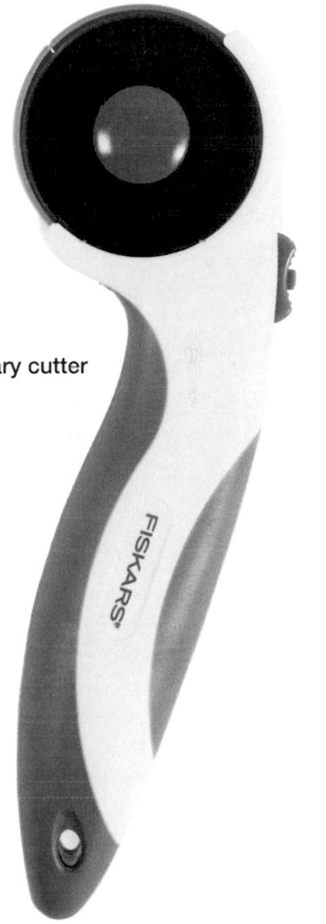

Rotary cutter

ROTARY CUTTERS AND MATS Unlike scissors, rotary cutters cut through multiple layers of fabric and pattern pieces without lifting the stack off the table. They also prevent layers from shifting, which can happen when a scissor blade slides under them. Blade diameters determine the handle size and range from ¾ inch to 2½ inches. Smaller cutters navigate tight curves, such as armholes or necklines. Larger cutters get through heavier fabrics, loftier thicknesses, and more layers, and they move effortlessly along a straight or moderately curved seam. Alternative cutting edges include rotary blades for pinking or scalloping, which are interchangeable and less expensive than corresponding shears.

Designed to protect your work surface and extend the life of your blade, cutting mats are printed with a right-angle grid and a 45-degree diagonal line for bias cutting. Mats come in a wide range of sizes and shapes. Unless it was designed to fold or roll, store your mat flat on a dedicated surface, hang it on a wall, or leave it where it's protected from extreme temperatures and buckling. To prolong the life of your mat, never iron on it.

Pins

Don't overlook the importance of the pin. Centuries ago, pins were so valuable that housekeepers locked them away and carefully dispensed them to only a select few. Today, there are many more varieties of pins than you would ever guess; choose and use them well. For detailed instructions on pinning your garments before sewing, see p. 112.

ANATOMY OF A PIN Pins are certainly not complicated, but when you become familiar with the weights, lengths, and heads available, you'll understand why the pins you choose make a difference in your sewing experience. **Lightweight pins** are labeled as "superfine" or "silk" and sometimes "0.5 mm." Expect a narrow pin with a sharp point. These pins glide through a double layer of fabric and a pattern tissue effortlessly. They're the pins experienced sewers prefer. **Normal, standard, midrange pins** aren't labeled as such, so you can expect any pin not otherwise marked to fall into this category. Although these pins work in most fabrics and are more reasonably priced than superfine pins, they generally don't pass through the fabric as easily. **Heavy-duty pins** work when your fabric is so heavy it bends regular pins, such as thick canvas or upholstery fabrics.

Lightweight pins

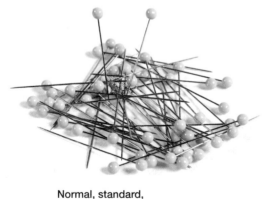

Normal, standard,
midrange pins

Heavy-duty pins

PIN SIZES Pin lengths make a difference too. Sewing pins range from 1 1/16 inches to 1 3/4 inches in length. You want good-quality, fine weight (usually), and the right length for your project or your preference. Long pins include the 1 1/2-inch size, which is one of the most popular for sewing. They are good for pinning long, straight seams and hem allowances. They can do the work of two regular pins. Don't use the 1-inch-long pins that come to you in new clothes or from the cleaners or the 1/2-inch-long pins used for crafting; they are not good for sewing.

Metal-head pins have a ball or disk of metal that forms a stop so the pin doesn't slide through the fabric. With this small head, you can pin a seam together without a large head distorting the fit. **Glass-head pins** are easy to see and handle, and they come packaged in one or assorted colors. **Flat-head pins** are long (1 3/4 inches), fine, sharp pins with heads that look like abstract flowers. They don't roll and are easy to see, and with some brands you can press over the heads without damaging your fabric. **T-head pins** are for rugged use, such as large home décor projects, or for heavy outdoor fabrics and open knits (the T-head won't slip through the knitting). They are generally too heavy for normal sewing. And you don't want to use plastic-head pins, which will melt on your iron during pressing.

Metal-head pins

Glass-head pins

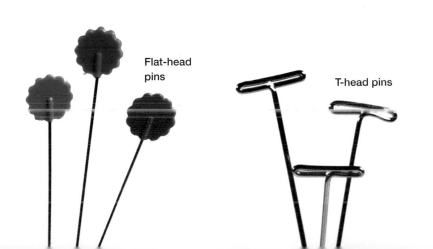

Flat-head pins

T-head pins

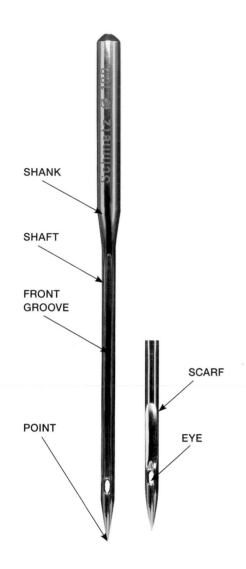

SHANK

SHAFT

FRONT
GROOVE

POINT

SCARF

EYE

Needles

For hand sewing, get yourself a variety pack of needles and experiment to find the size you're most comfortable with. As a general rule, use the smallest needle you can for your thread. For machine sewing, there are two factors to consider when selecting a needle: fabric and thread. Choose a needle style based on your fabric ("universal" is designed for most wovens, but you need special styles for other fabrics, like knits), then a needle size based on thread type. Following these guidelines helps ensure that the thread lays in the needle's front groove without wiggling and fits through the eye with little friction. If the needle is too large for your thread, your stitch may be uneven; if the thread is too large, it can shred or break. But when the needle is just right, the stitches form beautifully, as intended.

ANATOMY OF A MACHINE NEEDLE

Here are key features of a standard machine needle.

The **shank** is the needle top that inserts into the machine; most often it has a round front and a flat back, which seats the needle in the right position. The **shaft** is the needle body below the shank. The shaft thickness determines the needle size. The slit above the needle eye is the **front groove**, which should be large enough to cradle the thread for smooth stitches. The **point** is the needle tip that penetrates fabric to pass the thread to the bobbin hook and form a stitch. The point shape varies among needle types. The indentation on the needle back is the **scarf**; a long one

make it simple

Here's an easy way to keep track of which needle size is in your machine. Buy a tomato pincushion and use a permanent marker to label each section with a different needle type or size. When you remove a needle from your machine that isn't ready to be discarded, place it in the appropriate section. When you remove a needle from the cushion, place a glass-head pin in its place so you know what's in the machine.

helps eliminate skipped stitches by allowing the bobbin hook to loop thread more easily. A shorter scarf requires a more perfectly timed machine. The **eye** is the hole in the end of the needle through which thread passes. The needle size and type determine the size and shape of eye.

STANDARD MACHINE NEEDLES Standard needles are configured based on the particular fabric to be sewn. **Universal** is the safest choice for most fabrics. These needles have a slightly rounded point and elongated scarf for a foolproof meeting of needle and bobbin hook. **Ballpoint** needles are for heavier, looser sweater knits, whereas **stretch** are for highly elastic fabrics, such as Lycra®. Both have rounded points that slide between fabric threads instead of piercing them. **Denim** needles are meant for heavyweight denim, duck, canvas, upholstery, artificial leather, and vinyl. They have a deep scarf, acute point, and modified shaft to sew without pushing fabric into the needle-plate hole. **Microtex®** and **sharp** needles are intended for sewing microfiber, silk, and synthetic leather; precisely stitching edges; and heirloom sewing. They have an acute point.

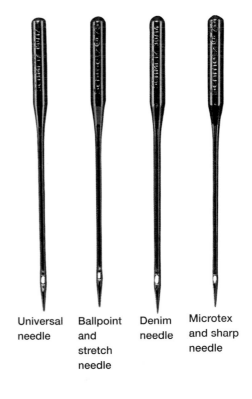

Universal needle

Ballpoint and stretch needle

Denim needle

Microtex and sharp needle

DECORATIVE MACHINE NEEDLES Decorative needles are configured to wed thread to fabric for surface embellishment. **Topstitching** needles have extra-large eyes and large grooves for heavy thread. **Embroidery** needles are meant for embroidering or embellishing with decorative thread. They have neither a sharp point nor a ballpoint; they are made with an enlarged eye to prevent threads from shredding or breaking and to prevent skipped stitches. **Metallic** (metafil and metallica) needles are for sewing with metallic threads. They have a universal or standard point; a large, elongated eye; and a large groove to allow fragile metallic and synthetic filament threads to flow smoothly.

Wrap a needle in tape or stick it in a cork before discarding.

Topstitching needle

Embroidery needle

Metallic needle

unconventional tools

You don't have to be wed to your local sewing-supply shop for tools and supplies—fantastic, inexpensive sewing finds show up in the most unexpected places. The grocery and hardware stores are favorite haunts, but you can also find items at the beach and even at your dentist's office.

From the grocery store

- **Plastic milk cartons** corral all sorts of sewing notions. Thoroughly clean 1-quart and 2-quart containers, cut off the tops, and nestle them in a deep drawer.

- **Sheets and drapes** usually come in clear zippered bags. Dump out the sheets and store everything you need for a project in the bag. You can easily identify the contents, your half-finished projects will stay dust free, and the bags stack nicely.

- **A picnic flatware** holder that sports vertical compartments and a handle is great for long, skinny tools like marking pens and rulers. The napkin-holder compartment fits notepads.

- **Pad an old fabric roll** or wrapping paper roll and wrap it in muslin, then use it for pressing seams in pants.

- **Make patterns from wax paper.** It's sturdy but slides beautifully over fabric. It's also semitransparent and great for tracing or positioning over prints. And, best of all, it's cheap! After you make your pattern pieces, simply store them in the empty cardboard roll. Wax paper also makes a superb stabilizer because it's stiff and slightly slippery but easily tears away.

- **Freezer paper** is just as fabulous as wax paper, but for different reasons: You can iron it directly to the fabric, so it holds the fabric in shape as you stamp, stencil, or silk-screen. It gently tears away when you're done.

- **A cleaning caddy**—a shallow bucket with a handle in the center—makes a great portable home for all sorts of cutting and marking tools: scissors, rotary cutter, ruler, French curve, pins, tape measure, pens, and pencils.

- **Place gripper shelf liner** on the table next to your sewing machine. You can then set bobbins, needles, and spools of thread on it without worrying about them rolling off.

- **Keep pins in little wooden dipping bowls.** Get five or six to keep in various areas of your sewing studio. They're easy to load and empty, and when one fills up, just rotate it to another spot in the room.

From the hardware store

- **Buy metal washers** to use as inexpensive pattern weights. They come in many sizes. Wrap them in muslin or pretty fabric to make sure the metal doesn't touch your fabric or pattern.

- **Plastic hardware trays** that are usually used to store nuts and bolts are great for pins, needles, and buttons. The plastic partitions move easily to accommodate different shapes and sizes.

- **Needle-nose pliers** are great for pulling needles through thick, heavy fabrics like leather and wool.

- **A telescoping magnet,** found at most auto-supply stores, makes easy work of picking up tiny bits of metal like pins and runaway eyelets.

- **An old toolbox** or picnic flatware holder corrals all sorts of pattern-drafting tools: pattern hooks, markers, awl, French curve, tracing wheel, mini stapler, shears, tape, and notcher.

From the vanity

- **Collect pretty hatboxes** and use them as decorative storage.

- **Invest in an assortment of inexpensive, funky makeup bags.** Group various items in each bag: buttonhole tools, marking tools, and so on.

- **Use coin purses** to store little notions, such as garment labels and hand needles.

- **Turn fabric tubes with a bobby pin.** Snip a hole ⅛ inch in from the edge of the tube, insert the pin into the hole, then pull it down the length.

- **Buy a set of makeup brushes** to clean the dust and lint from your sewing machine and serger. The small brushes get into all the nooks and crannies, and the large powder brush makes easy work of bigger surfaces.

From far and wide

- **Dental tools** from medical-supply stores (or ask your dentist) will greatly improve your sewing. They'll allow you to steer little bits of fabric under the presser foot, and they're wonderful for turning corners.

- **Pattern drafting requires a lot of paper.** Bulletin-board paper is just the ticket; one roll will last years. You can also use examining-room paper, which is available from medical-supply catalogs.

- **When you visit the beach,** collect various sizes of smooth rocks and use them instead of purchased pattern weights. Just make sure they have one flat side—then run them through the dishwasher to clean and disinfect.

- **Use wooden drawing figures,** sold in art stores, as mini dress forms. Drape little bits of muslin fabric on them to work out design ideas.

sewing machines

Your sewing machine is by far the biggest tool in your arsenal. Choosing the right one for you can be daunting. Prices range from just over $100 to well into the tens of thousands, and you can find them anywhere from department stores to specialty shops, as well as online.

Types of machines

There are four basic types of home sewing machines: mechanical, electronic, serger (also known as overlock), and embroidery. **Mechanical** machines are the least expensive, and you use manual controls to run them. **Electronic**, or computerized, machines have more power, capability, and longevity than their mechanical cousins, along with a larger price tag. Serger and embroidery machines are specialty equipment. The **serger** is designed for sewing stretchy fabrics and knits, using multiple needles and threads. **Embroidery** machines include special attachments that allow you to embroider (in addition to regular sewing).

Handy sewing machine features

Buying a sewing machine can be a big investment, so here are some features you should look for to make your sewing life a little bit easier.

AUTOMATIC NEEDLE THREADER Almost all machines include this; if you're eyeing one that doesn't, keep looking.

NO-SEW FEATURE If you're forgotten to lower the presser foot, this nifty warning light switches on and keeps you from ruining your stitching.

NEEDLE UP/DOWN SETTING Allows you to program your machine always to stop sewing with the needle in the highest position (to release the needle and bobbin tensions) or lowest position (to pivot easily and keep your fabric in place if you pause during stitching).

STITCH MEMORY Saves you time resetting the same stitch and ensures you're using the same settings throughout a project.

PRESSER FOOT KNEE LIFT When you need two hands to manage your fabric, you can use your knee to control the presser foot.

AUTOMATIC THREAD TENSION CONTROL Adjusts your needle tension based on the thread weight, stitch, and materials, but you can override this feature if you want to remain in control.

SPEED CONTROL For when you want to slow down and sew with precision. This is particularly helpful for beginners who are getting used to the foot control.

ONE-STEP BUTTONHOLE Even some experienced sewers avoid projects with buttons because they don't want to deal with buttonholes. This feature stitches a gorgeous buttonhole with just one click.

SPECIALIZED PRESSER FEET Older machines generally have two choices—straight and zigzag—but newer specialty feet make it easier to sew decorative stitches and seams.

LOW BOBBIN THREAD ALERT Sensors alert you when your bobbin thread is headed toward empty

how a sewing machine works

All sewing machines create a stitch by interlocking a top thread, threaded through the needle, with a lower thread, wound around a **bobbin** (1). The **needle bar** (2) holds and moves the needle. A **presser foot** (3) holds the fabric under the needle and keeps it flat against the **feed dogs** (4), which are small teeth that extend from the **throat plate** (5).

The **thread tension dial** (6) controls upper-thread tension. The **stitch width dial** (7) sets the distance the needle bar steps sideways. The **spool pin** (8) holds thread in place, and the **bobbin winding spindle** (9) winds thread onto an empty bobbin. The **fly wheel** (10), or hand wheel, turns as your needle goes up and down. The **stitch length setting** (11) controls the length of a stitch back to front, and **reverse control** (12) creates backstitching to secure stitches. Every machine can produce a straight stitch and most can create a buttonhole stitch; many models include additional utility and decorative stitches, which you can choose from the **stitch selector** (13).

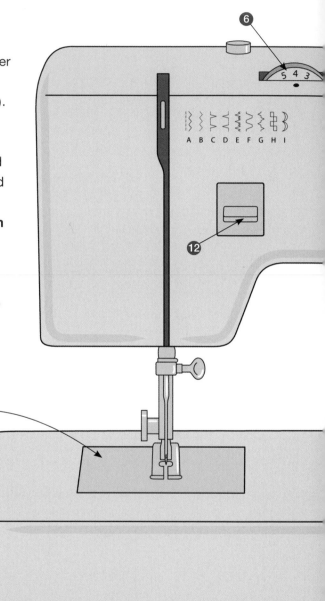

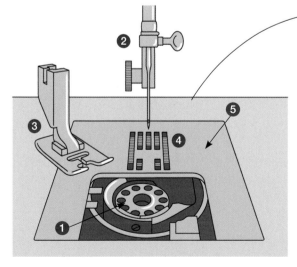

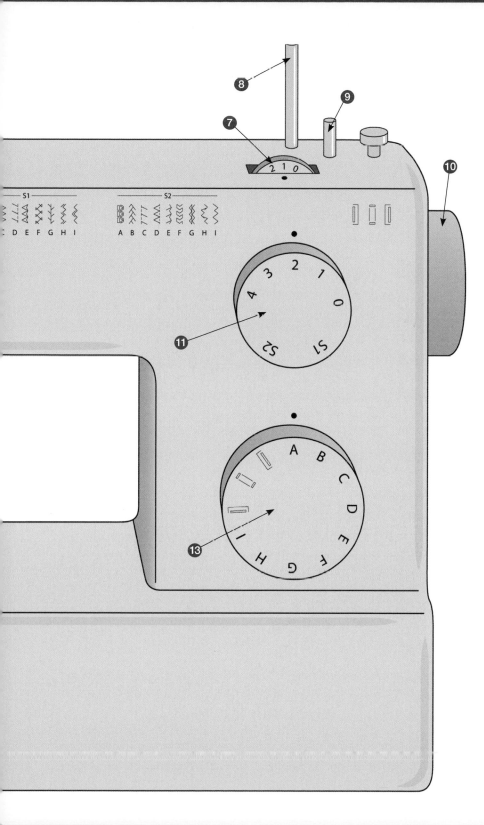

How is a stitch formed?

The formation of a stitch begins when the needle penetrates the fabric and descends to its lowest point. The bobbin then slides by the needle's scarf, catching the upper thread, and carries it around the bobbin and bobbin thread.

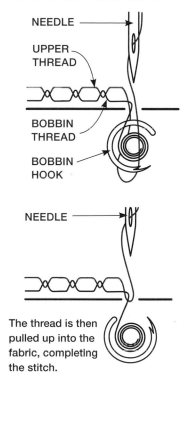

NEEDLE

UPPER THREAD

BOBBIN THREAD

BOBBIN HOOK

NEEDLE

The thread is then pulled up into the fabric, completing the stitch.

Care and maintenance

Once you've invested in a sewing machine, you'll want to follow these helpful guidelines to ensure your sewing success and the long life of your machine.

BEFORE EVERY PROJECT

- Change your needle. A worn, not-so-straight one can nick your throat plate or bobbin case.

- Make sure you choose an appropriate needle for your fabric and thread.

- Remove the throat plate and blow out lint. It accumulates between the feed-dog teeth.

- Take out the bobbin case and brush it clean.

- Clean the spool holders to make sure they are free of dust, lint, and stray threads.

Every three to four months, clean your machine thoroughly. Do this more frequently if you are having stitching problems. Before you begin, double-check your manual for particular instructions for your model.

EVERY SO OFTEN

- Remove foreign objects. Use a brush to get rid of lint, dust, threads, broken needles, and any decorative elements, like sequins. Canned air and mini vacuums are good for removing lint you can't reach.

- Dust the outside. Use a soft cloth and glass cleaner. To prevent future dust buildup, keep your machine covered when not in use.

- Wipe down the workings. Clean the needle bar and tension discs, and remove any adhesive residue from spool spindles, pressure feet, and the machine bed.

Oil (if needed). Some machines require regular treatments with oil; if yours does, do this after cleaning. Use only the oil recommended for your machine.

fabrics

Crisp, dry linen. Rich, buttery four-ply silk. Toothy, complex wool tweed. The fresh bouquet of a floral-print cotton lawn. All fabrics have their pros and cons. How do you choose the right one for a particular project? Handle it; compare it to others you like or dislike; and consider its color, texture, and weight as well as what it's made of and how it's made. But before you go shopping, familiarize yourself with basic fabric characteristics. As for prewashing, if you're going to launder your finished garment, wash and dry the fabric before you begin.

- -

Plant-based fabrics

Plant-based fabrics include cotton, linen, hemp, and ramie. They are strong, whether wet or dry, take dye well, and press nicely, but they soil and wrinkle easily and are prone to mildew. These fibers are dense and absorbent, but they don't wick moisture or dry quickly.

Animal-based fabrics

Silk, wool, and hair fibers (like angora, mohair, camel's hair, cashmere, and alpaca) are animal-based fabrics. They are usually lightweight, insulating, elastic, and able to absorb moisture. They resist wrinkling and take dye well, but certain insects adore munching on them.

Synthetics

Synthetic fabrics have come a long way over the years. Thanks to new fiber structures, fabric coatings, and more, man-made textiles are easy to care for and comfortable to wear. They are extremely resistant to wrinkles, soil, and water, and they wick moisture and have excellent durability and insulation.

Weaves and knits

While the fiber content of a fabric determines its overall feel, its weave structure contributes to its drape and stretch.

WOVENS

Woven fabrics are stable and have some give on the bias; they press and take creases cleanly. They don't have much stretch, so they offer support and can conceal bulges. If you treat a woven garment well, it will hold its shape over time and many wearings.

- **Plain** weaves, like muslin, consist of a simple under-over pattern of lengthwise and crosswise yarns. They tear easily along the grain and are prone to wrinkling.

- **Twill** weaves, such as denim, have a diagonal rib on the surface. They fray badly and can be bulky at intersecting seams.

- **Satin** weaves (which can include some cotton, wool, and synthetics) look glossy and smooth, but are susceptible to snags.

KNITS

Knits, which are made of interlocking loops of yarn, stretch and drape better than wovens. They mold closely to the body and forgive a less-than-perfect fit. Knits don't wrinkle badly, but they are hard to shape into crisp lines. Natural-fiber knits can sag and lose their original size and shape, and they shrink more than wovens. Knits with a small percentage of spandex fiber have improved strength, stretch, and recovery.

Nonwovens

Leather, suede, fur, felt, nonwoven interfacing, and paperlike specialty fabrics are nonwoven. Each has its own characteristics and sewing requirements, so be sure to have a little extra on hand so you can experiment before jumping into your project.

⎯🧵 fabric ideas

There are so many wonderful types of fabrics to choose from; these are just a sample of what's out there. Walk around your local fabric store and ask for suggestions, and you'll have no problem finding the perfect material to fit your needs.

Crinkled silk chiffon

Cotton sateen

Cotton twill

Tweed with
metallic thread

Polyester satin

Textured cotton

Mesh knit, sweater knit

Slinky knit

Textured knit, power knit

Shantung

Chiffon

Raw silk

Jersey

Four-ply crepe

Selecting fabrics

To find the right fabric for your design or pattern, ask yourself the following questions:

- Is it stable or stretchy?

- What is its weight and density?

- How well does it absorb moisture?

- Is it opaque or sheer?

- How does it drape?

- What is its surface texture?

- What is its color, pattern, or print?

There are no right or wrong answers, but your responses should help you determine whether the fabric is best for what you're planning. If a pattern is labeled "for knits only," you don't want to choose a woven. A clingy knit may work better than a loose cotton if you're envisioning a form-fitting dress.

Pairing fabrics

Putting different fabrics together really lets your creativity shine. When layering fabrics, try to select two that complement each other's strengths and weaknesses to create a beautiful, comfortable garment. Here are a few combinations that work well:

- **Linen and silk** Linen is easy to sew and comfortable to wear, but it wrinkles in a hot minute. Pairing it with a lighter-weight silk reduces the wrinkling.

- **Felted wool and knit** Jacket-weight textured wools can be scratchy next to the skin, but a layer of soft cotton or viscose knit makes it soft as a kitten.

- **Gauze and silk Dupioni®** Semisheer fabrics, like featherweight wool or cotton gauze, layer beautifully over silk Dupioni, providing additional coverage and a smoother texture.

secondhand fabrics

You don't have to turn your back on used fabric or yardage that has been lingering in someone's attic or a thrift shop. Here are some tips on finding and treating secondhand cloth.

Explore the thrift store

Antiques shops and flea markets are great places for treasure hunting.

Recycle linens

High-thread-count sheets can make beautiful nightgowns, robes, or curtains, or you can use them to make test garments or interfacing.

Make a trade

Get your sewing pals together for a fabric swap. Ask everyone to bring all the fabric they want to trade.

Get rid of mildew and stains

If your new find smells like mildew, wash it. If it has yellowed, lay it in the sun. If it's stained, try soaking it in an enzyme-based detergent for several days.

Eliminate bugs

Put all vintage wool fabric and garments in the freezer for a few days. Take them out for a day, then return to the frost for another two days. This kills any critters and their eggs.

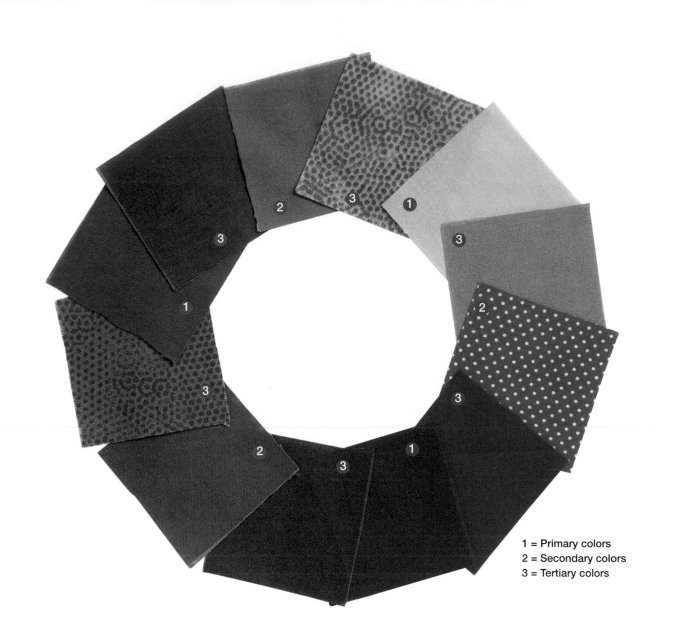

1 = Primary colors
2 = Secondary colors
3 = Tertiary colors

Choosing Color

Color is another important consideration. You already know what your favorites are, but you may hesitate when trying to decide how to put different hues together. The color wheel (above) represents all the hues in an orderly array.

You need to think about four color-related factors when looking at fabric. A successful color scheme will share at least one characteristic of the following: the hue (actual color), the temperature (warm or cool), the value (light or dark), and the intensity (bright or dark).

- **Monochromatic schemes** are made of colors that are nearly identical in hue but vary in value and/or intensity.

- **Analogous schemes** are made up of colors that are next to each other on the color wheel, like blue and purple.

- **Complementary schemes** juxtapose colors that sit opposite one another, like red and green. You can highlight or downplay the contrast by playing with value and intensity.

Estimating fabric yardage

Patterns frequently instruct you to use yardage of a particular size fabric. If your project calls for a specific width and you fall in love with a different size, don't despair—just use the following chart.

yardage conversion chart

To use this conversion chart, read across the row to determine how much material you'll need. For example, if a pattern requires 1 yard of 60-inch fabric and you want to use a 35-inch size instead, you need to buy 1¾ yards.

60 in.	54 in.	45 in.	35 in.
1	1⅛	1⅜	1¾
1⅜	1½	1¾	2¼
1¾	1⅞	2¼	2⅞
2	2¼	2¾	3⅜
2⅜	2⅝	3⅛	4¼
2¾	2⅞	3⅝	4¾
3⅞	3¼	4	5¼

threads

Choosing thread is not as simple as matching the color to your fabric: You also need to consider strength, colorfastness, and chemical resistance. Natural-fiber threads, such as cotton, linen, silk, and rayon, sew beautifully. However, synthetic fibers, like polyester, nylon, and acrylic, are stronger.

Monofilament thread

Texturized thread

COTTON THREAD is made from cotton fibers. It has little stretch, low sheen, and limited strength, and it can produce a lot of lint. It's best for lightweight natural fibers.

COTTON-WRAPPED POLYESTER THREAD is made by wrapping a continuous polyester filament with staple cotton, so it has the benefits of polyester and the look of cotton. It's best for all-purpose sewing.

POLYESTER THREAD is strong, colorfast, and resistant to ultraviolet rays, rot, mildew, and chemicals. It has some stretch and good recovery and is heat resistant. It's best for all-purpose sewing.

RAYON THREAD is made from a continuous fiber. It has no stretch and very little strength, and it is not always colorfast. It tolerates high temperatures and is soft and beautiful. It's best for decorative stitching and machine and embroidery; do not use for construction.

SILK THREAD is made of natural continuous fibers that are strong and smooth, with a lustrous sheen. It's best for hand sewing, tailoring, and basting.

NYLON THREAD is made from extruded filaments and comes in a variety of forms, all of which are strong and rot resistant. **Monofilament** is best for invisible sewing and blind hems. **Texturized threads** are best for serged seams, decorative sewing, and rolled hems. **Upholstery threads** are extremely strong and best for their namesake.

Upholstery thread

SERGER THREAD is finer than all-purpose thread. It's best for high-speed sewing.

ELASTIC THREAD has a continuous elastic core wrapped with thread. It's best for machine stitching and shirring.

Serger thread

TOPSTITCHING THREAD, also known as buttonhole twist or cordonnet, is available in silk, polyester, cotton-covered polyester, and cotton. It's best for heavy-duty utility sewing, open decorative machine stitching, bold topstitching, hand-stitched buttonholes, and cording machine buttonholes.

Elastic thread

METALLIC THREAD has a foil-like appearance and can separate, so stitch slowly, loosen the tension, use a larger needle, and pair with all-purpose thread in the bobbin. Best for decorative stitching and embroidery.

Topstitching thread

make it simple

If you find that your bobbins are unwinding and the thread tails are becoming tangled, try using stretchy ponytail holders. They fit snugly against your bobbin, and you can pick a color that best matches your thread so you can easily find the hue you need.

Metallic thread

hand stitches

Even in this high-tech age, you can't beat hand stitching and thread for some tasks. This timeworn combo is often forgotten in the modern world of elaborate sewing machines that can stitch, embroider, and quilt in every configuration imaginable. But with hand needles, you can control, ease, and secure your fabric better than with the fanciest of machine models. Here are four hand stitches you can use to construct a whole garment, plus four bonus stitches in case you want to crank your sewing up another notch. Use the smallest needle that fits your thread, but experiment to find the size that makes you most comfortable.

The first four stitches require a single length of thread and are meant for the right hand; if you're a lefty, simply reverse the directions. Always anchor your thread at the beginning and end of your stitching. (The only exception is the basting stitch, which is temporary.) All securing knots should be hidden between fabric layers or on the fabric's wrong side.

make it simple

For fast and easy needle threading, use a short length of thread to prevent tangles: The length of your forearm is a good measure. Coat the thread with beeswax, which straightens and strengthens it. Cut the thread on an angle, then wet with your lips. The thread should slide right through the eye of the needle.

Even in this high-tech age, you can't beat hand stitching for some tasks.

Easy knots

To begin, create a **slide knot**: Hold one thread end between your left index finger and thumb and the other end in your right hand. Wrap the thread two or three times around your left finger (not too tightly). Keeping the thread taut with your right hand, use your left thumb to roll the loops down off your index finger. Secure the entangled loops onto your thumb with your index finger, then use your fingernail to pull the tangles into a small knot.

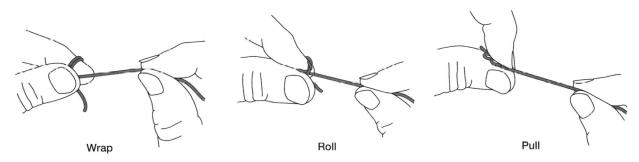

Wrap   Roll   Pull

To end, loop and pull: Catch one or two yarns of the fabric under the needle, then pull the needle and thread through until a small loop forms. Pass the needle through the loop and pull to knot. Repeat if desired. Cut the thread end close to the stitches.

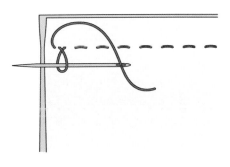

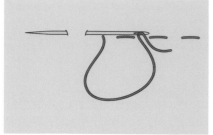

Basting stitch/running stitch

PURPOSE: To temporarily (basting stitch) or simply and securely (running stitch) hold fabric layers together

HOW TO DO IT: Insert the needle down into the fabric then up ¼ inch or ½ inch away. For a basting stitch, don't secure your thread ends.

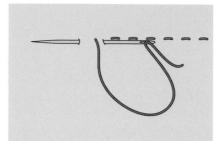

Backstitch

PURPOSE: To stitch permanent seams

HOW TO DO IT: Bring the needle up to the right side of the fabric. Sink the needle ⅛ inch to the right of the point where the thread emerges and up ¼ inch to the left of the point where the thread emerges.

Catchstitch

PURPOSE: To subtly and flexibly secure a hem or facing to a garment

HOW TO DO IT: Working from left to right but with the needle point facing left, catch a few threads of the garment fabric. Then move ½ inch to the right and catch the hem allowance.

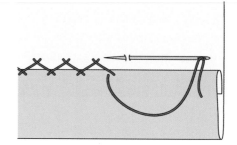

Slipstitch (aka blind stitch)

PURPOSE: To firmly and invisibly secure a folded edge

HOW TO DO IT: Come up through the folded edge and catch a yarn or two of the flat fabric. Then slide the needle under the fold for ½ inch to 1 inch. The thread is hidden in the fold.

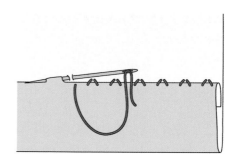

Bar tack

PURPOSE: To reinforce stress points, such as the corner of a pocket or slit

HOW TO DO IT: Use a doubled length of thread. Take two or three long stitches in the same place. Starting on one end, slip the needle under the stitches; catch the fabric underneath as well. Pass the needle back through the thread loop to form a knot.

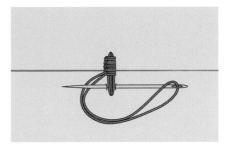

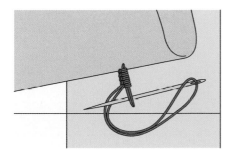

Swing tack

PURPOSE: To connect a lining to a garment while still allowing each to move freely; also called a *French tack*

HOW TO DO IT: Use a doubled length of thread. Take a small stitch in the garment then one in the lining, leaving about 1 inch of thread between the two layers. Starting on one end, slip the needle under the swinging threads. Pass the needle through the thread loop to form a knot.

Buttonhole stitch

PURPOSE: To fashion a handworked buttonhole or decoratively finish an edge

HOW TO DO IT: Use a doubled length of thread. Bring the needle up on the right side of the fabric ⅛ inch to ³⁄₁₆ inch from the cut edge. Pass over the edge, and bring the needle to the left of your first stitch. The spacing is your choice. Pass the needle back through the thread loop to form a knot.

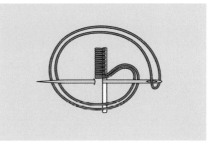

Understitch

PURPOSE: To add stability to inner layers and stabilize edges

HOW TO DO IT: Use a pickstitch, which is a tiny backstitch. With the inside of the garment facing you, place the stitches about ½ inch from the garment's edge and about the same distance from one another. Stitch through all layers except the outermost. You can use pins to mark even placement. Maintain even, dotlike stitches. If you draw the needle too far backward, you'll form a dash. If you don't go back far enough, you may go into the hole the thread came out of, and the stitches won't form.

machine stitches

Most sewing machines have a bunch of options for multiple stitches and effects, but you need to understand only a few basic stitches to complete most sewing jobs.

- -

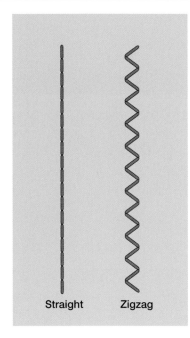

Straight   Zigzag

Straight stitch

PURPOSE: To make most seams and hems

ADDITIONAL INFO: The stitch-length selector (dial or lever) allows you to change the length of the stitch. A short stitch is best for sewing lightweight fabrics, a medium length is suitable for general sewing, and a long stitch is good for basting. Staystitching is a row of permanent, straight stitches on a curved edge (such as a neckline) to prevent stretching.

Zigzag stitch

PURPOSE: To prevent raw edges on seams from fraying and for edging, attaching elastic, and adding trim

ADDITIONAL INFO: This stitch binds threads while allowing for movement, so the thread won't snap and seams will not open. It's also good for joining pieces of fabric.

Overedge stitch

PURPOSE: To produce neat, durable seams on bulky fabrics and to prevent the edges of woven fabrics from fraying

ADDITIONAL INFO: This stitch simultaneously creates and finishes a seam. It's excellent on knit fabrics, like jersey, and is sometimes known as the overcast stitch.

Edgestitch and topstitch

PURPOSE: To finish and edge and to add a decorative element

ADDITIONAL INFO: The edgestitch is a functional stitch generally used to finish hems and is sewn $\frac{1}{16}$ inch to $\frac{1}{8}$ inch from the folded or sewn edge. The topstitch is a more decorative element sewn $\frac{1}{4}$ inch to $\frac{3}{8}$ inch away from the edge; you can use a contrasting-color thread as an accent.

Understitch

PURPOSE: To add stability to inner layers and stabilize edges

ADDITIONAL INFO: Stitch from the facing's right side through the facing and the seam allowances. Flatten the seam allowances as you sew and stitch slowly to stay $\frac{1}{16}$ inch to $\frac{1}{8}$ inch from the seam.

Lockstitch

PURPOSE: A straight stitch similar to the running stitch (see p. 38) to simply and securely hold fabric layers together

ADDITIONAL INFO: Like the running stitch, the thread dashes are end to end, but they touch. The sewing machine uses two threads that cross through the fabric to create a stitch.

basic machine sewing

Before you get started sewing, it's best to take a few driving lessons—both to make sewing easier and to improve your results. It takes a little practice to drive straight, navigate turns, take corners, jump bumps, and sew seams and edges that look the way they were intended to. Your success depends on how you use your hands to control the fabric as you sew.

It's important that you develop a feel for your sewing equipment. When you sew on a machine for a while, you become very familiar with the way it accelerates and how it sounds. You come to know its vibration, pings, and knocks, and you can hear when it's not running smoothly. Smooth sewing also depends on starting with a machine outfitted with the correct needle (p. 18) and thread (p. 34) for the fabric you're using.

Sewing straight lines

The long seams found on pants legs and the vertical seams on skirts and dresses should be straight and pucker free, with seam allowances that have a consistent width. Subtle changes in the width of multiple seam allowances around a garment can significantly change the garment's size.

Seam guides

FOLLOW THE SEAM GUIDES To help you stay on the road for even and accurate seam allowances, most machines have parallel seam guides engraved into the throat plate.

KEEP LAYERS MOVING AT THE SAME PACE When you're sewing through two or more layers of fabric, the bottom layer moves slightly faster than the top one, resulting in a misaligned seam. This is because the feed dogs grip and pull the lower fabric under the presser foot, but the presser foot creates a slight resistance on the top fabric. To keep both layers moving through the sewing machine at the same pace, drape a loop of fabric over your hand as shown at right.

PIVOT TO CORRECT Pivot the fabric with your hand, moving left or right, always keeping the fabric edge aligned with the seam guide while the machine stitches.

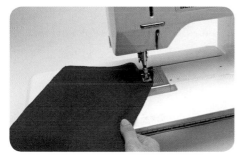

Steer the fabric in front of the needle.

Make steering corrections to keep the edge aligned with the seam guide.

Don't distort fabric to sew a curve.

Think of the fabric as flat paper as you drive through curves.

The right hand's fingers steer the fabric around the curve and to the right from behind the needle.

The fingers turn the fabric counter-clockwise for a convex curve.

Sewing curves

Improperly sewn curves can cause necklines that flare away from the body, and armholes that gape, are too tight, or have rough-looking, puckered, or angular edges.

DON'T GO STRAIGHT Problems occur if you distort the fabric as it goes through the needle in a way that changes the original shape of the curve. The tendency to straighten a concave curve as it is being stitched causes the curve to shorten, which can make a neckline or armhole too tight. A curve that was straightened during sewing (as in the top left photo) causes the curve length to shorten as on the armhole.

KEEP THE FABRIC FLAT The technique for driving around concave and convex curves is to sew them as if the fabric were a stiff, inflexible piece of paper. You can't stretch or bend the curve as you sew, requiring you to use your whole hand to control the direction of the fabric. One hand controls the fabric to maintain an accurate seam allowance, while the other hand gently directs the fabric through the arc of the curve. In all cases, when you're driving curves, use your hands and fingers to direct and follow the original shape. Here are some tips to sew it right:

- While keeping the fabric flat, drive it through a concave curve moving the whole cloth in the direction of the arrows.

- Sometimes steering around a concave curve occurs from behind the needle to keep the fabric flat and the seamline even.

- Your hands turn through a convex curve in the opposite direction. Keep your hands open to evenly distribute the weight of your fingers and to move the fabric gently.

Sewing sharp corners

There are all sorts of corners: 90-degree, 45-degree, and smaller; inside, outside, and inset. You see them on front openings, lapels, and pockets.

FOR PERFECT POINTS For a well-sewn outside corner, such as a collar point, add an extra step. Stop sewing the seamline a stitch or two before you reach the end point. With the needle down, pivot across the point, take two or three stitches, and pivot again to follow the opposite seam. Compare the points shown in the photo below right when the fabric is turned right-side out. The squared-off corner has a much sharper finished point than the corner that was sewn by pivoting at the point.

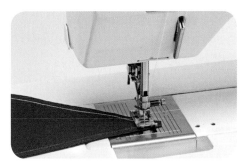

Stitch just shy of the corner, pivot, and take two or three stitches across the point.

Sewing a squared-off corner results in a sharp point.

Sewing a pointed corner results in a blunt point.

FOR INSIDE CORNERS Sewing a corner is often a matter of sewing along a line to a marked point, positioning the needle down into the fabric, lifting the presser foot, pivoting the fabric to the desired angle, lowering the presser foot, and resuming sewing. This method works best for inside corners or inset corners.

Inset corner

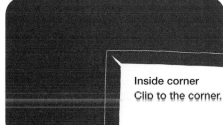

Inside corner
Clip to the corner.

When the presser foot isn't parallel to the feed dogs, the stitching goes wrong.

You can prop up the heel or toe of the foot until you stitch across the bump.

When the toe crosses the bump, it will need to be propped up until the whole foot has cleared.

Jumping bumps

When seams intersect with a waistband or hem, or you otherwise come to a point with a many-layered bump to sew over, it's easy to get high centered. When this happens, your machine usually jams at the top of the bump because the presser foot isn't perfectly horizontal. Most often, this results in a snarled mess of threads to cut out of your machine and your garment.

To drive over these bumps without skipping a stitch, keep the sole of your presser foot parallel to the feed dogs. To keep the presser foot level, use a folded scrap of fabric to raise the low end of the foot, as shown above. Stitch until the toe drops. Then position the scrap under the toe, and drag it along as you continue sewing until the heel drops.

Taut sewing

Taut sewing involves pulling the fabric forward and backward simultaneously as you sew, as shown below. This intentionally removes the slack from the fabric to produce an ultra-smooth seam or uniform topstitching on woven fabrics or to create a wavy, lettuce finish on knit or bias edges.

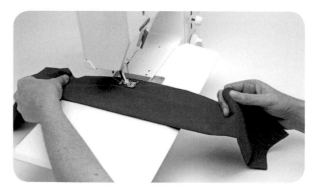

By maintaining an equal amount of pressure on the fabric as it passes under the needle, the feed dogs control the movement of the fabric as they should. However, if you pull the fabric too hard, you will overpower the feed dogs. This often causes the needle to break because the pressure on the fabric bends the needle, which then hits the throat plate and snaps. The goal is to pull the fabric in opposite directions enough to tighten it but not so much that you lose a neutral tension (meaning a balance of pressure in both directions). If you are in the habit of taut sewing all the time, stop—or you'll continue to break needles.

getting good tension

Good sewing machine tension produces smooth, even seams. If your tension isn't right, it throws off the quality of your stitch. Here are a few tricks to help correct it.

Sew it slanted

Cut a 5-inch to 7-inch on-grain (parallel to your fabric's tightly woven edge, or selvage) square from your fabric. Stitch a line of straight stitches from one corner to the opposite corner (on the bias). Hold the square at opposite stitched corners, and pull the corners apart until you feel the thread break.

See when it's wrong

If only one of the threads breaks—top or bottom, often in more than one location—that thread is too tight. Either slightly loosen that thread tension or slightly tighten the other thread tension.

Know if it's perfect

Examine the position of the broken stitches. If the top and bottom threads break in exactly the same location(s), you have perfect tension.

removing stitches

Sometimes stitches just have to come out. Ripping out a seam does not mean you are a poor sewer; it simply means you have an opportunity to try again and make it right. When unsewing, using the wrong technique can damage a garment. Overmanipulating a cut edge and stretching can make fabric splay at the seamline. This may distort the seam's shape, causing the new seam to look wavy or producing an uneven, puckered seam. Proper ripping techniques prevent distortion of the cut edge and damage to the fabric and set the stage for smooth stitch blending after the seam has been repaired. Once you know how to properly unsew a seam, you'll even be able to alter ready-to-wear garments with ease and quickly reclaim fabric from thrift-store finds to expand your sewing horizons.

Read the following tips before you remove a single stitch; they'll help you do the job right. *Remember*: Don't take your frustration out on the seam. It's best to adopt a calm, methodical approach.

- **Work under good light.** Use task lighting to help distinguish the stitches from the fabric. A magnifying glass with a light helps with dark fabric and short stitches.

- **Position the garment properly.** Turn it inside out, and position it so the cut seam allowance edge lies across your lap (perpendicular to your legs).

- **Clip the seam end stitches.** To prevent overripping, clip the first and last stitch in the area to be ripped.

- **Remove the cut threads.** To make the alteration or repair undetectable, remove all threads from the ripped area before you resew.

- **Match new stitches to the old.** When replacing the stitches, match the original stitch length and overlap seven stitches on each end, sewing right on top of the original stitch. Do not back-tack.

- **Use a lockstitch.** If the original seam was stitched with a chainstitch, replace it with a lockstitch (the straight stitch your machine makes).

- **Match your thread.** If an exact thread match is not possible, use a darker shade for better blending.

Ripping requires few tools, and they are relatively inexpensive. Sewing professionals rarely use seam rippers because they offer less control than other tools do. All the tools described here are extremely sharp and should be handled with care.

Embroidery scissors

For general ripping, look for scissors with a sharp point, a sturdy blade, and a large thumbhole.

Flat blade

Professional tailors use a flat blade because it allows them to cut quickly with superior control. Flat blades have to be sharpened with a sharpening stone.

Needlecraft scissors

For ripping smaller stitches, use these cutters with their fine point and sharp blades that can slip under even the shortest stitch without damaging the fabric.

Razor blade

The single-edge razor blade is available at hardware stores. Its short length and extremely sharp blade makes it difficult to control, so it's typically used only on garments sewn with heavy-weight thread.

Seam ripper

If you do use a seam ripper, look for one with a fine (thin) tip, and cut the stitches in a motion perpendicular to the stitch.

Ripping out a seam does not mean you are a poor sewer; it simply means you have an opportunity to try again and make it right.

hemming

Hems are some of the last details added to projects, and often we give them short shrift in order to get to the fun part—wearing the garment. After spending so much time and consideration cutting and sewing, why spoil all your hard work with the wrong hem for the job? Here are effective machine- and hand-sewn hem finishes that leave you plenty of time to show off your stylish efforts.

- -

Machine hems

For straight or slightly curved hems on woven fabrics, use one of the machine-sewn hems shown here. You can stitch them quickly on your sewing machine—with a little help from accurate pressing (p. 57).

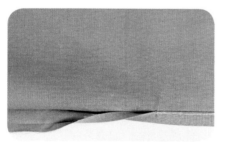

Turn under twice, and stitch.

DOUBLE-TURN AND TOPSTITCH A good technique for most casual garments is the double-turn and topstitch. For this finish, leave enough fabric to fold up (double-turn) twice. A typical hem allowance for shirts is ½ inch (for a finished hem of ¼ inch), while a hem allowance for jeans is 1¼ inches (for a finished hem length of ⅝ inch). Press up the full hem allowance, and then tuck under the raw edge to meet the fold; this creates a straighter hem. For shirts, spray the hem with starch and let it dry before you press it. Topstitch the hem close to the inside folded edge.

EMBELLISHED Use embellishment to create an adorned hem that also finishes the raw edge. Press a 1-inch hem allowance to the right side. Cover the edge with lace or ribbon that's at least ¼ inch wide (picot-edged trim is pictured here). Use a three-step zigzag stitch to topstitch the trim in place.

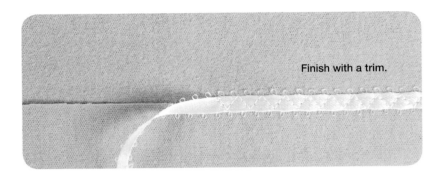

Finish with a trim.

CHIFFON A chiffon hem is best as an alternative to the rolled hem on transparent fabrics. Parallel to the raw edge, run a straight stitch ⅛ inch below the hemline. Fold the hem under on the stitchline, and edgestitch. Use small scissors to trim close to the edgestitching. Fold the edge under again. With the wrong side up, stitch on top of the first stitching. Overlap the beginning stitches with the ending stitches. Do not backstitch.

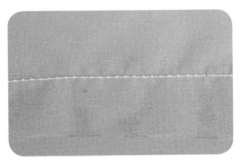

Stitch below the hemline.

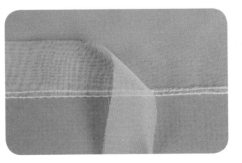

Fold, edgestitch, and trim.

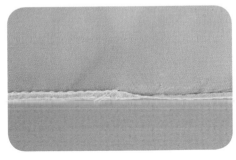

Fold and stitch again.

serger hems

If you have a serger, use these hems on wovens or knits when you want the hemstitching to be part of the garment's design.

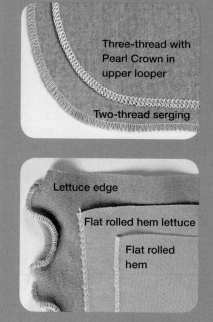

Three-thread with Pearl Crown in upper looper

Two-thread serging

Lettuce edge

Flat rolled hem lettuce

Flat rolled hem

Narrow edge

Also called an overedge, the narrow edge is mainly used for woven fabrics and is particularly attractive on wools. To sew it, set up your machine for two-thread serging, and stitch. If your serger doesn't have a two-thread option, use a three-thread narrow edgestitch and run Pearl Crown rayon in the upper looper.

Rolled hem

When rolling a soft, transparent fabric such as chiffon, set the machine for the widest cutting width possible, disengage the knife, and guide the fabric's raw edge to the inside edge of the presser foot. On knits, adjust the differential feed as needed: Use higher settings to keep the edge flat. Use lower settings and slightly stretch the fabric as you stitch to make a lettuce edge.

Cover stitch

Not all sergers can create a cover stitch, so double-check your manual. This stitch is a standard finish for knits. Press under a ½-inch- to 1-inch-wide hem allowance. Stabilize and secure it with a ¼-inch-wide strip of fusible web inside the hem. Set the serger for a cover stitch and stitch with the right side up. Align the stitch so the raw edge is enclosed under the stitching on the wrong side. If you don't have a serger, use a 3.0 mm twin needle on your sewing machine to achieve comparable results.

Cover stitch hem (wrong side)

Twin-needle hem (wrong side)

Fuse hem allowance with fusible tape.

Cover stitch hem (right side)

Fold under the raw edge and
hem allowance.

Sew with an edgestitch foot.

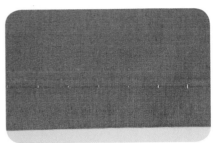

Finished blind hem (right side)

BLIND For a blind hem, press the hem allowance up, and then
press the raw edge under by ¼ inch. Fold the garment back,
exposing the folded hem edge an even ⅛ inch. Install a metal
edgestitch foot that has a skatelike blade. Guide the blade along
the garment fold to produce an even stitch. Set the machine to a
3.5 mm-wide, 2.5 mm-long slipstitch, and sew as shown above.

Facing, fusing, or binding a hem
Use the following finishes on curved or bias hems that tend to
pucker when turned up.

FACED HEMS Faced hems are best for garments made from
woven fabric. Cut or buy bias strips of a thin, tightly woven
fabric such as cotton broadcloth. Piece them to span the hem
circumference plus 2 inches. With right sides together, align the
strip along the hem. Overlap the strip past one side seam 1 inch,
and leave 1½ inches of the strip unstitched. Sew around the hem,
stopping ½ inch before the side seam where you started. Place
the right sides of the strip ends together at a 90-degree angle,
as shown. Stitch diagonally to join the ends and trim the excess.
Continue sewing the strip to the bottom edge. Press the seam
allowance toward the facing. Turn the facing to the wrong side,
bringing ⅛ inch of the fashion fabric with it, and press. Press the
facing's free edge under. Edgestitch the facing to the garment.

Sew trim in place.

Join the strip ends.

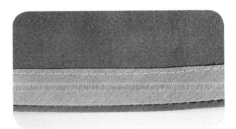

Edgestitch the facing.

FUSED HEMS Fused hems are best used on knit garments because the fusible tape stabilizes the stretchy hem for smoother sewing. Press the hem allowance under ½ inch. Insert a ¼-inch-wide fusible web strip under the raw hem edge. Fuse the hem in place. To maintain some stretch in the hem, finish from the right side with a zigzag stitch (1.5 mm stitch length, 1.5 mm stitch width) or with a twin needle.

Fuse the hem in place.

Zigzag hem (wrong side)

Twin needle (right side)

BOUND EDGE HEMS On heavy fabrics, use a bound edge hem. For wovens, cut a bias strip 1¾ inches wide by the circumference of the hem plus 2 inches. Press under one long edge ⅜ inch. Pin the strip's unpressed edge right side against the hem's wrong side. Overlap the strip past the side seam 1 inch, and leave the first 1½ inches of the strip unstitched. Stitch with a ⅜-inch-wide seam allowance, and finish the tape edge ends following instructions for the faced hem on p. 53. Press the seam allowance toward the strip. Fold the strip over the raw edge to the right side. Align the pressed strip edge along the stitching line, and edgestitch the bias strip.

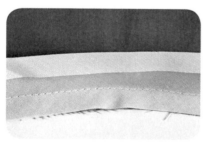
Attach a bias strip.

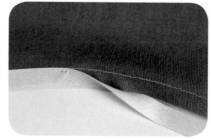
Fold the strip to the right side.

Stitch along the inner edge.

HAND-STITCHED HEMS Hand-stitch the straight hems of finer garments when you absolutely do not want see a stitch line. For all of them, use a single thread and a size 8 or 10 sharp needle.

Catchstitch For a catchstitch hem, press up the hem allowance and finish the raw edge with hem tape or by turning the raw edge under ¼ inch. Work from left to right (or right to left if you are left-handed). Catch a small stitch on the top of the hem allowance; then pick a small bite of the garment about ½ inch to the right. Your stitches will create a series of small Xs.

Slipstitch To make a slipstitch hem, press up the hem allowance and turn under the raw edge ¼ inch. Working from right to left, insert the needle inside the hem fold, out of sight, and bring it back out ½ inch to the left. Catch a couple of threads from the garment. Reinsert the needle into the fold and repeat.

Rapid stitch For a rapid-stitch hem, press up the hem allowance and finish the raw edge with hem tape or by turning under the raw edge ¼ inch. Position the hem vertically. Pick up a couple of threads on the garment; then pick a couple of threads on the hem allowance. Repeat, alternating between the hem and the garment to create a series of diagonal lines ½ inch apart.

Hems are some of the last details added to projects, and often we give them short shrift in order to get to the fun part—wearing the garment.

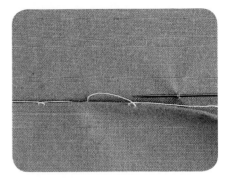

Bring the needle from left to right to form Xs.

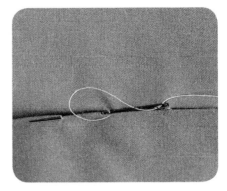

Slip the needle inside the folded hem edge.

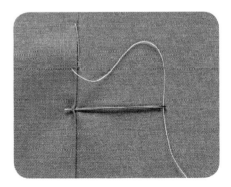

Stitch through the garment and hem with each stitch.

stabilizing tapes

When you're faced with puckered and stretched seams, wavy hems with peaks and pulls, and raveled and whiskered edges, you need help. This is where stabilizing tapes come in.

Sew-in tapes

Traditional sew-in tapes hold up well and are a great choice if you don't want to use fusibles.

- Tailor's stay tape Usually 100 percent cotton, ½-inch tailor's tape holds a seam to its intended shape and length. It's used to stabilize waistlines, necklines, shoulder seams, lapel roll lines, and gathered seamlines in tailored garments.

- Rayon seam tape This nonbulky, ½-inch-wide tape is used to bind raw edges to prevent raveling. It's a good lightweight alternative to tailor's stay tape.

- Petersham Also called grosgrain, its classic use is for hatbands or waistbands, but it is also used to reinforce seams or decorate edges. Petersham is heavier than tailor's stay tape and should be used on medium-weight to heavyweight fabrics.

Fusible stay tapes

Fusible tapes are the modern substitute for traditional tailor's stay tape. They are quicker to apply.

- Woven, straight cut This replaces cotton tailor's tape or rayon seam tape at necklines and seamlines.

- Woven, bias cut Because this is cut on the bias, it is flexible and easier to fuse to curves and other shapes.

- Tricot knit This tape is similar to bias-cut fusible tape, but is even more flexible and stretches while maintaining control. It is good for stabilizing seams and hems in knits and other stretch fabrics.

Fusible web

Use fusible web to hold hems, facings, collars, and zipper tapes or trimmings in place until they are permanently sewn. When the paper covering is removed from this tape, only a very sheer web of sticky glue is left. This is commonly used as an alternative to hand basting or to hold two fabric pieces together until you can complete stitching.

pressing

Did you know that ironing and pressing are two entirely different actions? It's true. Ironing is a sliding-back-and-forth motion intended to smooth out fabric. For example, you iron a blouse when you take it out of the dryer. Pressing, however, plays a more important role than merely eliminating wrinkles. Pressing is when you move the iron up and down to shape fabric and prepare for the next step of construction. Ironing can stretch fabric, whereas the point of pressing is *not* to stretch it. Pressing is probably the least understood aspect of sewing, and most sewers rush through it (or neglect to do it altogether).

When creating a garment, you may have to spend as much time at the ironing board as at the sewing machine. Seams, edges, hems, darts, and facings are all pressed at some point during construction. If you don't bother to press your fabric as directed, your finished project will not look half as good as it could. But don't moan and groan: Pressing is one of the easiest skills to master. You just need to know how an iron works, what your fabric requires, and a few tricks for getting the best results.

How an iron works

A standard household steam iron has a temperature control and a steam control. It also contains an internal water tank. When set to steam, the tank releases water, which hits the hot soleplate and converts to steam. This activity all happens inside the iron. The steam is then emitted through the holes in the iron's soleplate. The soleplate temperature must be at least 300°F for steam to form. If the iron is set to steam but the temperature is less than 300°F, water may dribble or spit from the soleplate and spot your fabric.

INTERNATIONAL CARE SYMBOLS FOR THE IRON

• **One dot** Use a low iron temperature (150°F to 250°F) for synthetic, thermoplastic hydrophobic fibers. (Steam will not be produced in this temperature range on most irons.)

•• **Two dots** Use a medium iron temperature (300°F to 325°F) on hydrophilic fibers such as wool, silk, and rayon. (Steam is produced in this temperature range on all irons.)

••• **Three dots** Use a high iron temperature (400°F to 450°F) for hydrophilic fibers such as cotton, linen, and ramie. (All irons produce good steam at this high setting.)

What your fabric requires

There are two major groups of fibers: those that occur in nature and those that are manufactured (see p. 27 for more). Natural fibers include cotton, wool, silk, linen, hemp, and ramie. These fabrics generally tolerate medium- to high-heat settings. Manufactured fibers include rayon, Tencel®/lyocell, acetate, and triacetate and those from petroleum derivatives, such as nylon, polyester, acrylic, olefin, modacrylic, and spandex. With the exception of rayon and lyocell, manufactured fibers are heat sensitive. When the iron's heat setting is too high for these fibers, they begin to soften and glaze. The fabric develops a hard, shiny finish and eventually melts and sticks to the soleplate.

Manufactured, heat-sensitive fibers must be pressed at lower heat settings at which steam usually cannot be produced,

The greatest damage to irons comes from dropping them. Be sure to handle yours with care.

but because most of these fibers absorb water poorly, they are best pressed with a dry iron anyway. Spandex is a heat-sensitive fiber that tolerates medium heat, but it too requires a dry iron. Remember, no fabric benefits from continuous steam—it must be allowed to dry for the pressing to set.

Getting good results

The three components of pressing are heat, moisture, and pressure. Good pressing results when the iron is set to the right temperature for the fiber and used with or without moisture to apply pressure to the fabric.

HEAT   Heat settings that home sewers use most range from 175°F for extremely heat-sensitive fibers to 450°F for linen. Most irons have a control dial marked with fiber names to adjust heat settings. Match the heat setting on your iron to your fabric.

MOISTURE   Delivered as a spray, sprinkle, or steam, water must be applied to fabrics made of hydrophilic fibers—those that require moisture for an iron to eliminate wrinkles or set creases. However, if moisture is put into the fabric but is not dried as part of the pressing process by finishing with a dry iron, the slightly damp garment will wrinkle again because the fabric has absorbed moisture and has not been properly dried. Allow pressed items to cool before moving them. Conversely, hydrophobic fibers don't need moisture because they don't easily absorb it, so water has no influence on wrinkle removal or crease setting. For example, there is no benefit to using steam with a polyester fabric; a warm, dry iron is sufficient.

PRESSURE   Pressure, which helps set creases or smooth wrinkles, comes from the weight of the iron and the hand of the user. The ideal weight of an iron is a matter of personal preference, but if you can comfortably lift a 4-pound to 4½-pound iron, you won't need to exert as much pressure when you're pressing. The weight of the iron does some of the work for you.

Are you pressing or ironing? Pressing is an up-and-down motion. Ironing is a sliding back-and-forth motion.

a guide to the basics: mending, hems, and buttons

For people who love clothing and textiles, few things are more disheartening than discovering that a favorite garment needs to be mended or hemmed or is missing a button. And if you aren't sure how to make the necessary repairs, these pieces serve as a silent reproach as they pile up in the closet corners. Doing these tasks yourself will save you time and money, and you can also improve the look of your skirts and pants or replace plain buttons with decorative ones.

Mending

When evaluating garment damage, first determine whether mending is possible and if it will save the garment. A mend may be possible if the damage is to elements of a garment's construction, such as released seams or darts, loose buttons, worn buttonholes, loose beads or sequins, tired elastic, a broken zipper, or a fallen hem or cuff. Mending also is possible if the damage is to hidden elements, such as shabby lining, or a hole in an inside pocket, under a button, or in a sock. A mend may not be possible if the damage involves the textile itself, such as rips and tears or insect damage in the body of the cloth, deterioration, shattering, or loss. Here are a few common damages that are easily repaired. Be sure to use mending materials that are equal or similar to the garment's fiber content and weight.

- **Restore with felting** Select a wool yarn that matches the fabric's color, then unravel and pull it apart to create loose fibers. Place a piece of polyethylene foam, such as Ethafoam® under the hole. Use a felting needle from the fabric's right side to work the fibers into the material. Trim and continue to work the fibers until they match the surface.

- **Repair holes from pulled-through buttons** Make a fabric patch slightly smaller than the button. Use a similar fabric, equal to or lighter in weight than the garment. Baste the patch to the garment's wrong side or between a facing and the outer fabric. Work machine darning or hand running stitches across and slightly beyond the patch, stitching through the patch and the

garment. Reattach the button with a reinforcing button underneath that is slightly larger than the patch.

- **Close split seams** Working on the garment's wrong side, press the seam closed. Trim any loose threads. Replace the seamline's missing stitches with a machine stitch or hand backstitch that equals the original seam's stitch length. Overlap existing stitches, taking care to sew through the original holes. Press the seam back to its original finished position.

- **Fix drooping sleeve hems on bag-lined jackets** If a jacket or coat sleeve hem is not attached to the fashion fabric, it will eventually droop. To fix this, release the lining, and press out creases on the fashion fabric. Return the garment cuff or hem to its original correct position, and gently press and stitch the hem allowance in the right place using a catchstitch. Then press the lining to remove creases, and return it to its correct position. Use slipstitches to reattach it, making sure there is a soft fold at the bottom for ease. Press gently.

- **Restitch a worn buttonhole** Trim any loose threads or frayed fabric. Baste a small matching fabric patch that is equal to or lighter in weight than the garment under the worn buttonhole. Using thread that matches the fabric, work neat rows of small running stitches through all layers across the patched area. Restitch the buttonhole through the patch, overlapping the previous stitching. If sewing by hand, cut open the buttonhole before stitching; if sewing by machine, recut the buttonhole after it is sewn.

Straight skirt and trousers: 2 inches

Gored or basic A-line skirt: 1½ inches

Moderately full skirt: 1 inch

Very full skirts, preserged or zigzagged: ½ inch

Fixing Hems

Hemming is a necessary part of creating a garment. Hems prevent the edges of fabric from fraying and create weight so clothing drapes properly. To make a single-fold hem, fold the edge over, press it, and edgestitch at the top of the fold. A double hem is created the same way, but you fold over the edge twice (this provides extra insurance that the hem won't ravel). For more on hemming your garments, see pp. 50–56.

It's not always easy to find garments that are the right length, particularly if you are petite or tall, and taking your clothes to a tailor can get pricey. Use the following formulas to hem skirts and pants to perfection.

- **Skirts** When an A-line or flared skirt's hem is too deep, the wider hem allowance gathers into the narrower skirt and causes a wrinkled and bulky-looking hem. This bulky hem is particularly noticeable after pressing. To avoid the problem when there's too much fullness, reduce the hem allowance until the fullness is minimal. The greater the curve, the narrower the hem allowance.

- **Pants** Many women's pants (and pants patterns) are created for an average-height woman wearing a moderate heel. If you prefer stilettos or ballet flats, you may want to alter your pants for a better fit. A pants' hem width should equal half the circumference at the bottom leg edge. The narrower the pants leg circumference and hem width, the shorter the length must be.

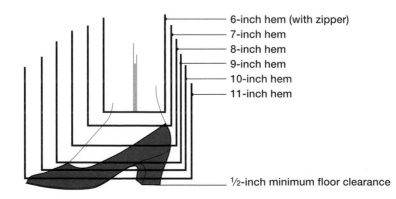

6-inch hem (with zipper)
7-inch hem
8-inch hem
9-inch hem
10-inch hem
11-inch hem

½-inch minimum floor clearance

Buttons

Replacing missing buttons is a necessary part of life, but you may also want to swap out existing plain-vanilla buttons with something more fancy. When sewing buttons onto lightweight to medium-weight fabrics, use a double strand of the same all-purpose thread you used to sew the garment. For heavyweight fabric, use a single strand of heavy-duty buttonhole twist or carpet thread. To prevent tangling and to give extra strength, coat the thread with beeswax and press it lightly with the tip of your iron.

Thread the needle and knot the ends together, if using a double strand. At the button mark, insert the needle between the garment and the facing to hide the knot (if there is no facing, insert your needle on the right side of the fabric to hide the knot between the fabric and the button). Take one or two tiny stitches through all the fabric layers to anchor the thread, and position the button over the stitches.

Bring the needle up through one hole and down through another, sewing through all the fabric layers. Repeat. For a two-hole button, sew five times. For a four-hole button, sew three times through each pair of holes. Secure the thread between the garment and facing (or under the button on the fabric's right side).

It's important to put the right size button in the right place, particularly on the front of a blouse, jacket, or coat. A pattern envelope tells you what size button to use. When a designer chooses the button size for the pattern, he or she designs the front edge based on that button size. The recommended button size should fit exactly between the front edge fold, or seamline, and the center front line. Check your button with your pattern by placing the button between the center front line and the garment front edge. If the button edge touches both lines without crossing either line, it's the right size.

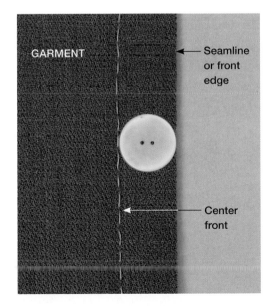

GARMENT

Seamline or front edge

Center front

pattern-free projects

Sewing without a pattern is the perfect way to get your feet wet without having to follow too many instructions and guidelines. With some basic tools and fabric, you can sew a garment with little fitting and no fuss.

* ❀ *

This chapter is divided into three sections: "Good to Start With," "When You're Getting Comfortable," and "If You're Feeling Inspired." You can work your way from the simpler projects to the more challenging ones, or just dive into the first one that catches your eye.

All sewing projects, no matter how easy or complex, require the same basic stuff. We call these supplies "The Usual Suspects." You won't use every tool for every project; read ahead, as you would with a recipe, to see what's needed.

the usual suspects

- ❏ Fabric
- ❏ Matching thread
- ❏ Measuring tools (ruler, measuring tape, seam gauge, yardstick, French curve)
- ❏ Cutting tools (shears, scissors, rotary cutter and mat, seam ripper)
- ❏ Needles and pins (thimble, pincushion, beeswax)
- ❏ Iron

sundress

what you'll need

The Usual Suspects (see p. 65)
1½ yards of fabric
Fitting buddy or dress form
Interfacing

This versatile sack dress starts with just a tube of fabric, then adds pleats, tucks, and wide straps. Printed cotton is a great choice, but the dress also looks great in softer, drapey fabric—just cut a little wider and use more pleats to create volume.

1 Measure bust, waist, and hips. With a measuring tape, measure your bust, waist, and hips. Note the largest of these measurements, and cut a rectangle of fabric approximately 20 inches wider than that measurement. Piece your fabric as necessary to get this final width.

2 Sew a tube. Measure from right above your bust to the dress length desired, and trim to this length, plus a little extra (so you can tweak the hem later, if needed). Sew the fabric into a tube, as shown below left.

3 Pleat on a dress form or body. Try the tube on or place it on a dress form that is your size. Pleat out the fabric at the front and back of the tube until it fits snugly against your body or form. The dress pictured sports a wide box pleat, but you can pleat any way you like. Mark the edges of the pleats with pins.

4 Add a top band and straps. Measure along the top edge of the pleated dress. Cut two strips of fabric that length, plus seam allowances, by 6 inches deep. These are the bands. Cut two 5-inch-wide straps, sew into tubes, and turn. Sandwich the straps between the bands on the front and back, and sew through all layers. Align raw edges with the pleated edge and sew, wrong sides together.

5 Sew on a wide hem band. Cut one 6-inch- to 8-inch-wide hem band the length of the hem circumference plus seam allowances. Sew the short ends of the band, right sides together, forming a ring. Fold in half lengthwise and press. Stitch to the dress's hem edge, then press the band down.

SEAM

RIGHT SIDE

BOX PLEAT

STRAP

BANDS

HEM BAND

placemat purse

What You'll Need

The Usual Suspects (see p. 65)

Placemat

1½-yard-long cord

Size 16 or 18 denim needle

A button or other embellishments

Fashion-forward and adorable, these little purses take just a few hours—or less—to sew. Starting with a ready-made placemat gives you finished edges and lining, which saves a ton of time (you can find cool ones at an import store). Choose a placemat that can be folded easily and doesn't have stiff or thick edges, as you'll have to sew through four edges and a cord. Use a size 16 or 18 denim needle; sewing through all those layers can break a smaller needle.

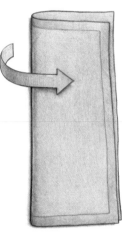

1 Fold the placemat in half lengthwise with wrong sides together, as shown. Press the fold.

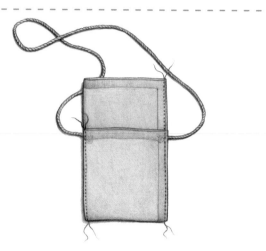

3 Knot the cord ends and bury them inside the seams; topstitch the sides of the purse to close them, as shown. Reinforce the stitching at the cord and the corners.

4 Fold the top flap down over the inside pockets and press the fold.

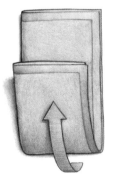

2 Fold one short end toward an imaginary line located about one-quarter of the total length of the placemat. Press the fold.

5 Add buttons, snaps, tassels, **or other** embellishments as desired.

reversible
chair covers

What You'll Need

The Usual Suspects (see p. 65)

¾ yard decorative fabric for
the main side

¾ yard decorative fabric for
the reverse side

Want to give your dining area a unique style for any occasion? A reversible chair cover lets you go from breakfast chic in pretty cotton to dinner elegant in gold satin. Easy to sew, with just a few seams, chair covers are a quick and economical way to transform a room. Choose a unique brocade for an elegant celebration, a whimsical cotton print for a day of make-believe, or a modern home décor fabric for everyday style.

Choose, measure, and cut the fabric

Reversible chair covers enable you to get two looks in one. The two sides can be different materials but should be close in weight. Prewash the fabrics before cutting if you want them to be machine washable after construction.

1 Select two middleweight to lightweight fabrics. The materials should not be too lightweight (you don't want show-through) or too heavy (to avoid bulky covers). The cover is completely reversible, so the two sides do not have to coordinate in color.

2 Determine the chair back width. Measure the chair back's widest point and add the chair back's depth (see right). Add 2 inches for seam allowances and ease.

3 Measure the chair back height. Starting at the bottom of the chair back, measure from the seat to the top of the chair and add half of the chair back depth, plus a 1-inch seam allowance.

WIDTH

DEPTH

HEIGHT

4 Cut the covers. Cut two rectangles on grain from each fabric, using the height and width determined in steps 2 and 3. If the fabric has a motif, be sure to center it.

Sew the covers

A few simple seams make these stylish and practical covers. The seams are enclosed, so they are left unfinished. All seam allowances are ½ inch wide.

5 Sew the seams. With right sides together, align, pin, and sew the top edge of the first fabric, then press the seam allowances open. Repeat this for the second fabric (the cover's reverse side). Next, with right sides together, align, pin, and sew the side seams on the first fabric. Repeat on the second fabric. Press open the side seam allowances.

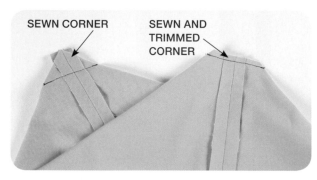

Sew the top and side seams.

6 Sew and trim the corners. At each corner, align the top-edge seam with the side seam. Sew perpendicular to the seams the depth of the chairs. Press and trim the seam allowance.

SEWN CORNER   SEWN AND TRIMMED CORNER

Sew the corners the length of the chair depth. Trim the seam allowance.

OPENING

Sew the lower edge, leaving a 7-inch to 10-inch opening.

7 Sew the covers together. Turn one cover right side out and place inside the other cover, so the covers are right sides together. Align and pin the lower edges. Sew three-quarters of the way around, leaving a 7-inch to 10-inch opening for turning (see photo above).

8 Through the opening, turn the chair cover right side out. Press the seam allowances to the inside. Hand-sew the opening closed (A) or topstitch around the lower edge (B). Press all the seams.

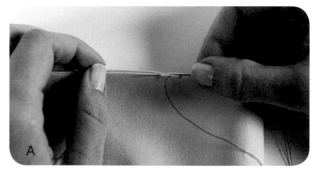

A

Turn the cover right side out, and hand-sew the opening.

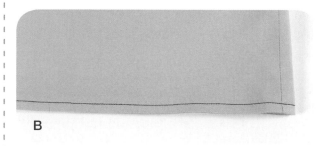

B

Finish the cover by topstitching around the lower edge.

decorative options

These covers are the perfect canvas for showing off your home-decorating style.

Piece it together. Give your covers an artistic look by piecing together fabrics before constructing the covers.

Add a ruffle. Before sewing the lower edge, insert a ruffle trim made from one of the fabrics or a coordinating fabric.

Tie it up. Before sewing the side seams, add self-fabric or ribbon ties. This is especially helpful to give the cover shape if the chair back is much wider at the top than at the bottom. Note that if the ties are large, they may be difficult to hide inside, so you may want to use only one side and have the other side serve as a lining.

flouncy tee

What You'll Need

The Usual Suspects (see p. 65)

T-shirt

You can take a T-shirt from baggy and unisex to fitted and flattering with just a few snips and seams. This style uses a curved peplum ruffle (made from the sleeves) to add interest to the sides and the back, and a draped collar to soften the tee's hard edges. You'll need a shirt that fits or is a little big. You can leave the edges raw (most jerseys won't ravel) and let them curl, or you're free to hem them if you prefer. This garment works best with T-shirts made of 100 percent cotton jersey. A stretch straight stitch or a narrow and short zigzag stitch is your best bet for seaming knits, unless otherwise indicated. This draped-collar tee is made from only one shirt, but you can combine two recycled tees to create a contrasting peplum and collar.

1 **Prepare the shirt. Remove the sleeves** and neckline. Be careful not to cut into the sleeves, as you will be using them for the ruffle. Trim off the bottom hem, or remove the stitching if the shirt is short. To reshape the bottom hem, fold the shirt in half, with the center front (CF) to your right and center back (CB) at your left. Mark the waistline on the shirt's CB fold with a

pin. Draw a line from this point, perpendicular to the CB, 3 inches to 4 inches long before curving it gradually, to the bottom edge of the shirt. Be sure your line crosses the side seams and stops 3 inches to 4 inches from the CF. Compare the width of your sleeve to the length of the revised hemline. If the hemline is longer, shorten it to match the length of the sleeve. Cut on the line you drew; this piece will become the draped collar.

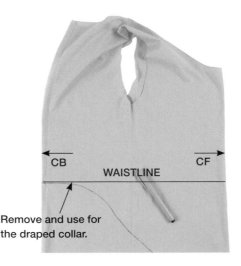

Remove and use for
the draped collar.

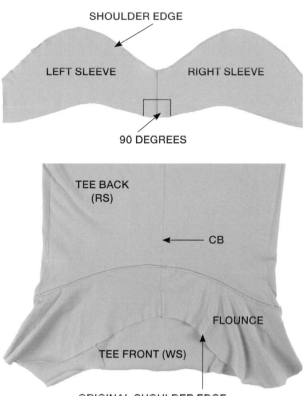

SHOULDER EDGE

LEFT SLEEVE   RIGHT SLEEVE

90 DEGREES

TEE BACK
(RS)

CB

FLOUNCE

TEE FRONT (WS)

ORIGINAL SHOULDER EDGE

Join the removed sleeves, and attach them to the hem for a flounce.

2 Make the peplum ruffle. Open the underarm sleeve seams, and remove the hem with a seam ripper to maximize the length. Fold each sleeve in half, and reshape the bottom edge into a gentle curve. Sew the two sleeve pieces, right sides together, along one of the underarm seams to make one continuous ruffle (see photo above, top). With right sides together, align the ruffle seam to the CB along the shirt's bottom edge, and continue to pin the ruffle to the curved T-shirt edge. Sew the curved seam.

3 Make the draped collar. Measure the circumference of the neckline. Then measure the length of the collar piece cut from the bottom of the shirt. Cut off the pointed ends so the collar piece length equals the neck

circumference plus 1 inch. Sew the two ends, right sides together. Match the collar seam to the CB and align and pin the collar's straight edge to the neckline. Stitch around the neck circumference.

Attach the collar piece to the neckline to create a draped look.

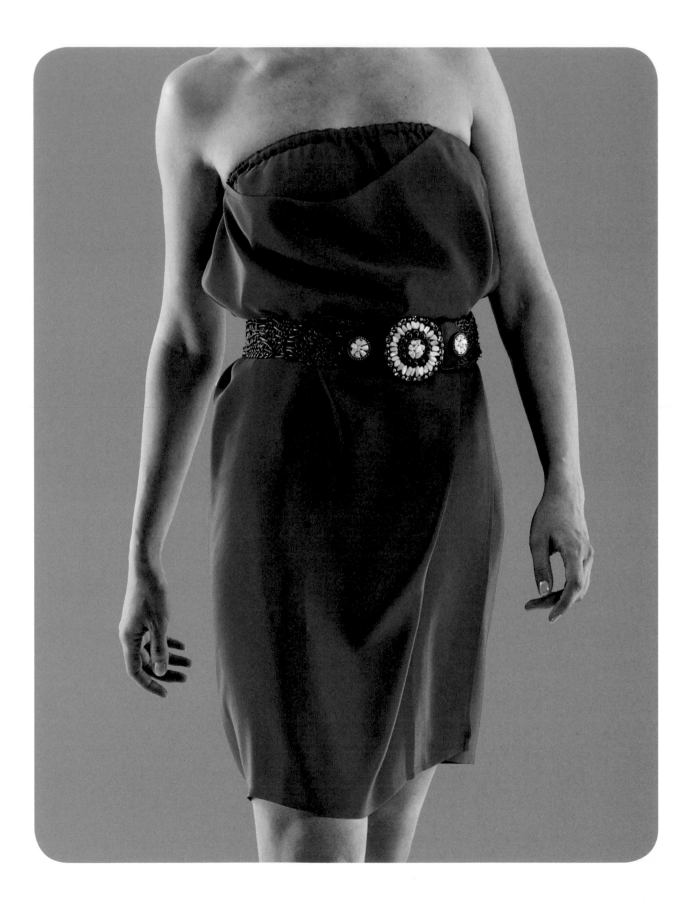

one-rectangle dress

What You'll Need

The Usual Suspects (see p. 65)

1 yard of 60-inch-wide fabric or 1⅔ yards of 45-inch-wide fabric

Safety pin or bodkin (a tool for threading elastic through a casing)

Point turner

½-inch-wide elastic cut 2 inches shorter than your waistline

This kicky strapless dress, which you can also wear as a skirt, is made from one rectangle. Use a drapey fabric such as 3-ply or 4-ply silk, rayon crepe, or lightweight wool. The garment shown is medium size, based on a 36-inch bust measurement. Add or subtract 2 inches from the width measurements for each size change. Lengthen or shorten as desired.

1 Double-fold a ¾-inch hem allowance. Sew ⅜-inch finished hems on two short edges and one long edge of the skirt.

2 Finish the remaining top edge if it is not the selvage edge. Sew a 23-inch-long, double-fold, ⅜-inch-wide hem. Backstitch at the inside end of the hem. Clip to the last stitch so the remaining fabric is able to lie flat.

3 Topstitch the remaining upper-edge section into a ⅝-inch casing for the elastic. Feed the elastic through the casing and stitch it at each end to secure.

4 Overlap the casing ends to form the waistband. Stitch them together, allowing the nonelasticized edge to drape.

Double-fold the hem.

Secure the elastic.

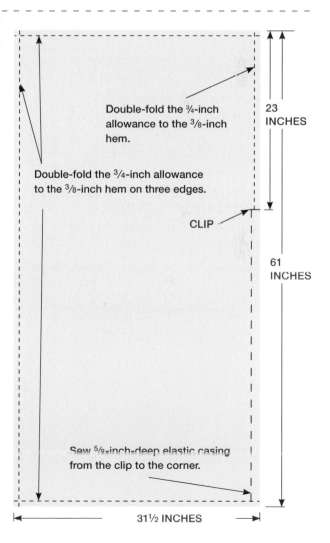

Double-fold the ¾-inch allowance to the ⅜-inch hem.

Double-fold the ¾-inch allowance to the ⅜-inch hem on three edges.

23 INCHES

CLIP

61 INCHES

Sew ⅝-inch-deep elastic casing from the clip to the corner.

31½ INCHES

convertible dress

What You'll Need

The Usual Suspects (see p. 65)

About 4 yards fabric with two-way or four-way stretch (look for at least 20 percent stretch; the size 10 dress shown here required about 4 yards of 53-inch-wide fabric)

Safety pin or bodkin (a tool for threading elastic through a casing)

½-inch-wide elastic (long enough to fit around your waist)

Pattern paper

Foamcore

In less than an hour, you can make a dress to wrap, roll, and twist any way you like. This dress has two extra-long, wide straps sewn into the front waistband. Wrap and twist the straps to form sleeves or straps, and a sash around your waist. Shift the waistband above your bust for tunic options, too. You've never seen so many styles for so little sewing. The dress is made from four geometric shapes with dimensions based on your measurements: a skirt, a waistband, and two long fabric rectangles that wrap, twist, and tie to become a bodice, straps, or sleeves. If you leave the edges unfinished, it can be a two-seam project, with only a waist and a skirt seam to sew. The version shown here has rolled serged edges.

Plan the dress, cut the pieces

Simple geometric shapes are the basis of this dress. Use the illustration for guidance as you apply your own measurements to design the pieces.

1 Plan the skirt. The skirt is two half-rings of fabric, like two doughnut halves. Divide your waist circumference by 3.14 to find your waist diameter. Divide the diameter by 2 to get the radius. Use the radius to draw the inside (waist)

semicircle, then add the desired skirt length for the outer hem semicircle. To make a "compass," lay pattern paper over a sheet of foamcore board, and stick a tack or pin in the middle. Place the eyelet end of a tape measure over the pin, and extend the tape measure out to the required length. Rotate the tape measure around the pin, marking the desired circle as you go. Add a ½-inch seam allowance to the edges.

Skirt

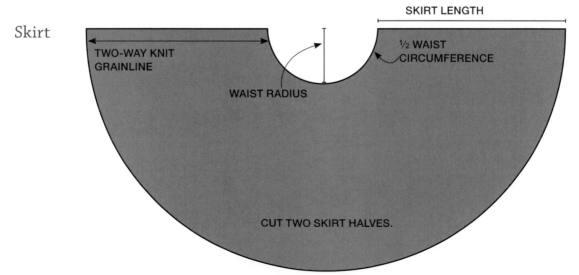

SKIRT LENGTH

TWO-WAY KNIT GRAINLINE

½ WAIST CIRCUMFERENCE

WAIST RADIUS

CUT TWO SKIRT HALVES.

Strap

BUST
CENTER
TO
UNDERARM

TWO-WAY KNIT
GRAINLINE

CUT TWO
STRAPS.

1½ TIMES THE WEARER'S HEIGHT

2 Determine the strap size. The two straps are identical rectangles. For the strap width, measure from the center of your bust to just under your arm. The strap length is one and a half times your height (add a few inches to the length if you're fuller-figured than average). The straps are cut so the stretch is parallel to the short ends.

3 Cut a waistband casing. Cut a band about 2 inches wide and a few inches longer than your waist measurement. Cut the band to stretch lengthwise.

Waistband (not to scale)

WAIST CIRCUMFERENCE PLUS 3 INCHES

2 INCHES

FABRIC STRETCH

CUT ONE
WAISTBAND.

TWO-WAY KNIT
GRAINLINE

Sew it together in three seams

To construct the dress, sew the skirt side seams. Then overlap the straps at the center front. Sew on the straps and a waistband in a single seam. Sewing the waistband and straps to the skirt is easier if you sew with the skirt wrong side out.

4 Finish the strap edges. Use a rolled serged edge or a narrow hem on the long edges of each strap.

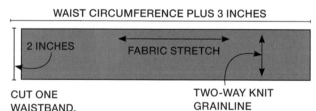

Try a rolled serged edge on the strap edges.

5 Sew the skirt seams. Pin the skirt's vertical edges together with right sides together, and serge or sew the seams. Fold the skirt to align the seams, then find and mark the center front and center back.

6 Place and pin the straps to the skirt waist. Align the straps' raw edges with the skirt waist, right sides together. Place the straps to overlap 3 inches to 4 inches, with the middle of the overlap at the center front. Pin or baste the straps in place; the waist curvature will cause the overlap to form a deep V-shape.

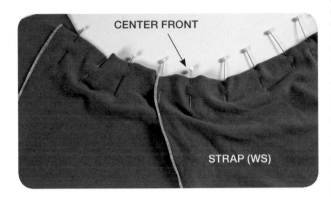

8 Add waist elastic. Cut an elastic strip to fit your waist, plus 1 inch. Run it through the waistband with a safety pin or bodkin. Sew the strip ends together and overlap the fabric to cover the elastic.

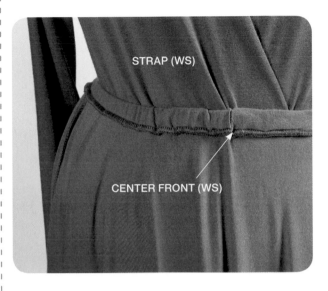

7 Sew the waistband casing to the skirt. Fold the waistband in half lengthwise, right side out. Align the band's lengthwise raw edges with the waist and straps' raw edges (the waistband should sandwich the straps against the skirt's right side). Serge or sew through all layers. Overlap the casing slightly when you complete sewing the waist.

9 Start wrapping and wearing. Both straps are sewn into the waistband seam. Wrap them over your shoulders and around your waist to achieve many possible styles.

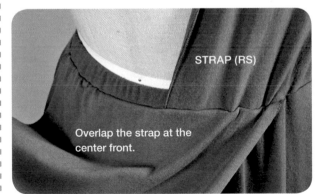

Overlap the strap at the center front.

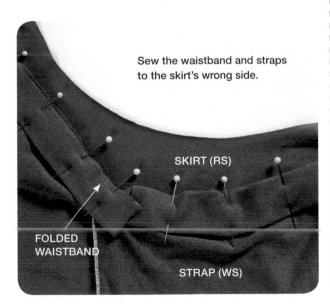

Sew the waistband and straps to the skirt's wrong side.

four-rectangle tunic

What You'll Need

The Usual Suspects (see p. 65)

1 yard of 60-inch-wide fabric

¼ yard fusible interfacing
for knits

6 buttons

This loose-fitting, soft tunic stitches up beautifully in any stretch knit or velour, and you can add a funky or classic touch with your choice of buttons. With some basic tools and a modest amount of fabric, you can sew a garment in a few hours with little fitting and no fuss.

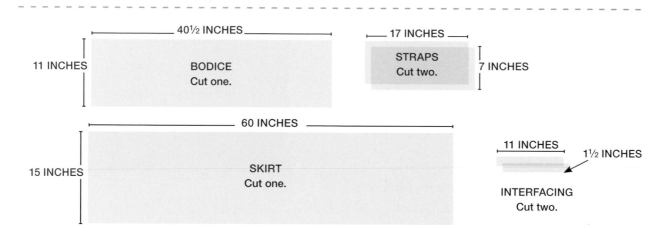

40½ INCHES

11 INCHES

BODICE
Cut one.

17 INCHES

STRAPS
Cut two.

7 INCHES

60 INCHES

15 INCHES

SKIRT
Cut one.

11 INCHES

1½ INCHES

INTERFACING
Cut two.

1 Add center-front support. Fuse the interfacing (follow manufacturer's instructions) to the wrong side of each center-front bodice edge.

2 Press under a ½-inch hem on the skirt. Topstitch.

3 Gather the top edge of the skirt to fit the bottom edge of the bodice. With right sides together, sew the skirt to the bodice.

4 Press the center-front edges of the bodice/skirt under 1½ inches. Topstitch.

5 Stitch four buttonholes in the right front of the bodice and two in the skirt. Sew corresponding buttons on the left front.

6 With right sides together, sew the long edges of each strap together to make a tube, and turn them right side out. Center the seam on the center underside of each strap. Gather the strap ends to a 2-inch width.

7 Try on the tunic. Mark the strap placements and check the strap length. Adjust as needed.

8 Turn under ½ inch at the top edge of the bodice. Pin the straps in place. Topstitch along the top of the bodice, catching the straps in the stitching.

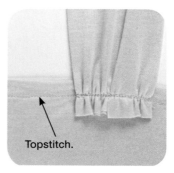

Topstitch.

gypsy skirt

What You'll Need

The Usual Suspects (see p. 65)

1 yard to 2 yards fabric, depending on the style you choose

1-inch or 1½-inch elastic

Safety pin or bodkin (a tool for threading elastic through a casing)

Horizontal bands of fabric are gathered and pieced together to make the foundation of this fun layered skirt. The bands can be various widths and lengths to change the fit and look. Use ½-inch seam allowances throughout, unless otherwise indicated. A double-fold hem finishes it. Subtle changes to the bands, and the number of bands you use, turn the skirt into different garments.

1 Cut the bands. Measure your largest circumference, probably your hips, and the length you want for your finished skirt. From these two measurements, you can determine the size to cut the fabric bands. The length of the horizontal band is the longer dimension of the band. Start with the top band, which will cover

Cut the bands based on your length and circumference measurements and the desired fullness.

the waist and hips. Cut it 7 inches longer than your largest circumference. If the measurement is longer than the width of your fabric, piece the band. The width of the band is the shorter dimension and is measured vertically on the skirt. Add 3 inches to the top band width to allow for 1-inch-wide elastic; for 1½-inch-wide elastic, add 4 inches. Plan the rest of your bands based on the gathering ratio you want for your fabric. Always add 1 inch to the width and length of each band for the seam allowances. Cut your bands on the cross-grain of the fabric; piece the fabric together to make the bands long enough.

Gather the lowest band to fit the one above it.

2 Sew the bands into rings. When you've cut and pieced each band, sew the two short ends of each band together in a seam, with the right sides together, to make a ring. Baste the top edge of each ring (except the top band) for gathering. Mark the rings in quarters, and pull the gathering threads.

3 Join the bands. Taking two adjacent bands at a time, align the quarter marks of the bottom edge of one band to the gathered top edge of the band that goes below it. Align the edges with the right sides together and distribute the gathering evenly. Sew them together as described in "Understanding Gathering" on p. 87.

4 Create the waistband.
The 3-inch extension added to the width of the top band forms a casing for a strip of 1-inch-wide elastic. Make this a double-fold edge.

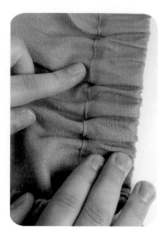

Fold the top edge under ½ inch, and press a crisp edge. Fold it under a second time 1⅛ inches, and press again for a double-fold edge. Edgestitch the casing. Leave a 3-inch section open at the center back to insert the elastic.

Insert the elastic into the casing. Use a large safety pin or a bodkin to thread the elastic through the casing. Overlap the two ends, and sew them together before pulling them into the casing. Edgestitch to close the opening.

Topstitch vertically. Stitch across the elastic at each side of the skirt so it won't roll or twist inside the casing.

six skirt variations

Now that you understand the gypsy skirt, you can change it slightly to make a variety of garments.

This tea-length version has an extra band, which makes the hem especially full. The top band was cut wide to keep that section slender.

The top band on this short skirt was cut narrow so the overall skirt would have more ease and be fuller.

The bands in this skirt are made of crisp fabric cut narrow, with a gathering ratio of 3:1. This makes the skirt look like a tutu.

This is the same skirt pattern with the casing worn above the bustline and straps added. The bands are varied colors to define the dress sections.

The three bands were cut with a slight gathering ratio of 1.5:1 for a lean, columnar look.

The top band was cut extra wide to extend below the hip, and a band with a ratio of 3:1 was added at the hem.

understanding gathering

To gather fabric, first sew a straight-stitched line by hand or machine across the area to be gathered. The machine gives better control. Then pull the thread to make the fabric gather, sliding it with your fingers. The more you pull the thread, the tighter you'll make the gathers. The ratio of the ungathered fabric length to the finished, gathered length determines the fullness of the gathers. The best ratio depends on the fabric you're using and the look you want. Test-gather a strip of your fabric to find the perfect ratio for the look you want.

No gathering The ratio here is 1:1. With no gathering, this fabric will hang flat on the body, but ease needs to be added for comfort.

1.5:1 Here you gather half again as much into the finished length. This is a soft gather and works for fabrics with more body than sheer or gauze fabrics.

2:1 With this ratio, you double the length of fabric to the finished length of the band. This provides an ample amount of gathering for lightweight fabrics and plenty of fullness for the skirt.

3:1 This is an extreme ratio and creates a lot of fullness. If the fabric has body of its own, this amount of gathering will make it wide, but in a soft sheer fabric it can drape elegantly.

1. **Baste a line.** Use a long stitch setting. Be wise, and stitch a double line in case one of your threads breaks while you're gathering. Sew one line just shy of the seamline and the other ¼ inch away in the seam allowance.

Sew two parallel lines.

2. **Pull a thread.** Pull the bobbin threads, and allow the fabric to gather on the thread. Keep sliding the fabric along the bobbin thread until the gathered section is the right length. Distribute the gathers evenly.

Pull the bobbin threads.

The gathers will continue to slide on the bobbin thread until they are secured by sewing over them. When you're making a gypsy skirt, sew one gathered band edge to another ungathered band edge.

3. **Pin the edges together.** Align the raw edges, right sides together, and pin them perpendicular to the edge.

4. **Sew with the gathered band on top.** This way, you can make sure the fabric stays exactly where you want it during stitching. Set the machine for a standard stitch length, and sew just to the left of the gathering stitches, so they won't show in the finished seam.

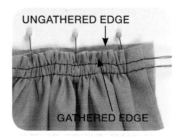

UNGATHERED EDGE

GATHERED EDGE

floor cushion

What You'll Need

The Usual Suspects (see p. 65)

2 yards 54-inch-wide home décor/upholstery fabric

6 yards soft cellulose cording

25 inches no. 4 or no. 5 cushion coil zipper and slider

24-inch-square boxed pillow insert or foam block with Dacron® wrap

Sewing machine zipper foot

Sticky notes

Expand your seating options and accent your décor with comfy floor cushions. A boxed cushion is comfortable and elegant, and simple to make without a pattern. Fabric-covered cording along the seams gives a professional look and reinforces the cushion's shape. Choose easy-care natural- or synthetic-fiber materials, such as cotton twill or canvas, polyester microfiber, leather-look vinyl, or fade- and stain-resistant indoor/outdoor fabrics. These instructions show you how to sew the most common size box cushion: 24 inches square and 4 inches deep.

Prepare the cushion pieces

The shapes for the cushion cover are simple squares, rectangles, and bias strips, and the dimensions are determined by the cushion size you want to make. The cutting diagram at right provides a layout for 54-inch-wide fabric and dimensions for a 24-inch square, 4-inch-deep boxed cushion cover. You can adjust the dimensions if you'd rather make a smaller or larger boxed cushion.

1 Mark the cutting lines. Unfold the fabric, right side down, to its full selvage-to-selvage width. Measure and mark the cutting lines on the fabric according to the diagram. Cut the pieces as marked. Write the code letter (A, B, C, etc.) or part name of each piece on a sticky note and affix it to the proper fabric piece to keep the pieces organized. Serge or zigzag-stitch all the cut edges, except the bias strips (E) and the two zipper boxing strips (B).

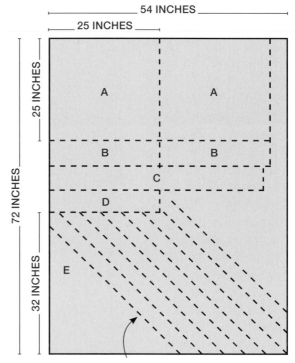

BIAS PIPING STRIPS

A. Top/bottom: Cut 2, 25-inch squares.

B. Zipper boxing strip: Cut 2, 5 inches by 25 inches.

C. Front boxing strip: Cut 1, 5 inches by 49 inches.

D. Side boxing strip: Cut 1, 5 inches by 25 inches.

E. Bias piping strip: Cut 7, 2 inches by 30 inches to 36 inches.

CUTTING LINES	- - - -
MEASUREMENTS	⊢—————⊣

2 Prepare the zipper boxing strips. Fold the 5-inch by 25-inch zipper boxing strips (B) in half lengthwise, wrong sides together. Serge or zigzag the raw edges together.

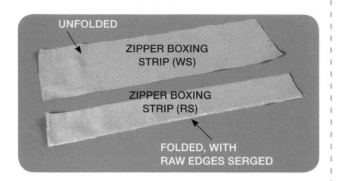

UNFOLDED

ZIPPER BOXING STRIP (WS)

ZIPPER BOXING STRIP (RS)

FOLDED, WITH RAW EDGES SERGED

3 Create a continuous bias strip for the piping. Position one strip (E) right side up and align another strip perpendicularly over the first strip's end, wrong side up. Stitch diagonally across the ends; press the seam allowances open and then trim. Sew the remaining strips in the same way until you have a 6-yard- to 7-yard-long bias strip.

4 Cover the cording. Lay the bias strip right side down. Center the cord on top of the strip, then fold the fabric strip lengthwise over

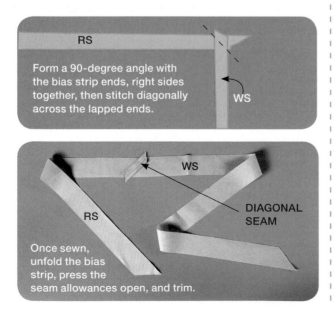

RS

Form a 90-degree angle with the bias strip ends, right sides together, then stitch diagonally across the lapped ends.

WS

WS

RS

DIAGONAL SEAM

Once sewn, unfold the bias strip, press the seam allowances open, and trim.

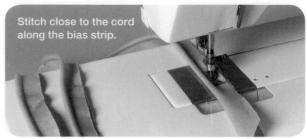

Stitch close to the cord along the bias strip.

the cord, enclosing it. Pin the fabric along the cut edges. Attach a zipper foot to your sewing machine and stitch the fabric strip closed around the cord; stitch close to the cord.

Assemble the cushion cover

Decide which of the cushion's four sides will house the zipper; the piping should begin and end on the same side as the zipper. Use ½-inch-wide seam allowances throughout. If you're using

a cushion zipper, attach a slider and stop to prevent the slider from slipping off during cushion construction. For the zipper stops, cut two strips of fabric and stitch one to each end of the zipper.

5 Sew the piping to both cushion faces (A). Cut the piping ½ inch longer than needed, then cut away ½ inch of the cord from inside one end. Fold this end's covering back on itself by ¼ inch, wrong sides together, and press. Position this end 2 inches from a corner, and align the piping flange with the cushion's face edge. Pin the piping around the cushion face. Begin stitching the piping 1 inch from the corner. Before you reach the corner, stop with the needle down, raise the presser foot, and clip into the piping flange ½ inch to ¼ inch to help the piping conform to the corner. Drop the presser foot and stitch the piping in place around the corner. Stitch the piping around the

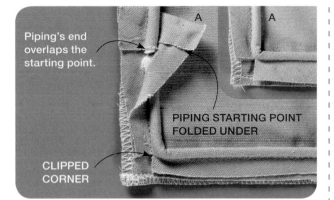

Piping's end overlaps the starting point.

PIPING STARTING POINT FOLDED UNDER

CLIPPED CORNER

remaining sides, clipping the corners in the same way. Before finishing, open the piping covering at the starting point and lay it flat. Lap the piping's end over the starting point, wrap the starting point's piping to cover over it, and stitch in place.

6 Create the zipper boxing. Attach a zipper foot to your sewing machine. With the zipper closed, align the folded edge of one zipper boxing strip (B) along the center of the zipper teeth or coil. Sew ⅜ inch from the folded edge along the length of the zipper and zipper boxing. At the zipper slider, raise the presser foot and shift the slider out of the way. Sew to the zipper's end. Repeat on the opposite side (see below).

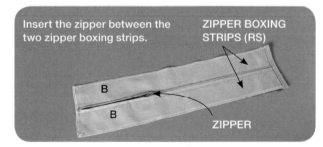

Insert the zipper between the two zipper boxing strips.

ZIPPER BOXING STRIPS (RS)

B

B

ZIPPER

7 Sew the boxing strips into a continuous band. Pin one short end of boxing strip C to one short end of boxing strip D, right sides together, and sew. Then, pin one end of the zipper boxing strip to boxing strip C's free end, and the other end of the zipper boxing strip to boxing strip D's free end, right sides together, and sew.

Sew the boxing strips together, end to end, to create a continuous band.

ZIPPER BOXING STRIPS

C

D

8 Attach the boxing band to the cushion faces. Pin the band to one cushion face (A), right sides together. Place the zipper closure on the same side as the piping's joined ends, and align the band's seams with the cushion face's corners. Mark all cushion corners on the band, or snip into the seam allowance. Sew all four corners of the band and cushion face together first, then open the zipper and stitch along each straight edge of the boxing band and cushion face. Sew the boxing band to the second cushion face.

9 Refine the seam. Sew around all four sides of the boxing band and cushion faces again, stitching close to the piping. This tightens the piping and conceals its stitching lines.

10 Complete the cushion. Turn the cushion cover right side out. To insert the cushion filler, fold it in half and slide it through the zipper opening. Unfold the filler and make sure its corners are aligned with the cushion's cover's corners. Fluff and close the zipper.

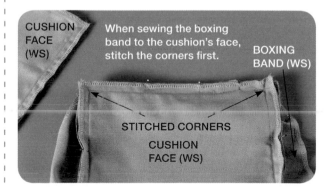

CUSHION FACE (WS)

When sewing the boxing band to the cushion's face, stitch the corners first.

BOXING BAND (WS)

STITCHED CORNERS

CUSHION FACE (WS)

3

working with patterns

Don't be intimidated by patterns. Creating a garment without one is a wonderful process, but working with a pattern means you're using a proven template that will create a great-looking finished product. Aside from the pattern department at your local fabric store, you can find a whole universe online and in books and magazines.

- ❊ -

If you live for Fashion Week but are on a limited budget, you can make up-to-the-minute, just-off-the-runway ensembles at a fraction of the price you'd pay in the store (and you can choose your colors and customize with your own special touches). And if you're flipping through a family photo album and find yourself craving a dress your grandmother wore, vintage patterns are a wonderful way to put together a garment from another time.

understanding patterns

Before you get started working with patterns, you need to understand the language. Here is a quick primer, including sizing and cutting terms and how to read the markings on the pattern tissue.

Sizing

Pattern sizing is different from ready-to-wear sizing. (Warning: Pattern sizing is always bigger.) Big pattern companies list sizing charts in their pattern books or on their websites. Independent pattern manufacturers might follow slightly different conventions. To determine your correct size, you'll need accurate body measurements (see p. 98 for more).

JUNIORS The size range for youthful figures with slim hips, smaller busts, and less waist definition. This fit reflects the sizing convention in junior ready-to-wear, but the numbers are different.

PETITE Sizing for women under 5 feet 4 inches with short limbs and torsos. Most juniors'-, misses'-, and women's-size patterns are "petiteable"—that is, the pattern pieces have handy lines indicating where you can shorten the overall length.

MISSES The size range for well-proportioned, developed figures with more pronounced curves through the bust, waist, and hip. Again, the fit reflects misses' ready-to-wear but with different size numbers.

WOMEN'S Sizing for the larger, fully developed, mature body (with bust measurements 38 inches or more).

PLUS SIZES For 40 inches or more at bust, 33 inches or more at waist, and 42 inches or more at hip.

Cutting

The first stop on most pattern instruction sheets is the cutting directions. They tell you how to lay out each pattern piece on your fabric and how many of each you need to cut.

WITH-NAP LAYOUT Nap is the direction in which raised fibers lie on the surface of fabrics like velvet, corduroy, and chenille. Nap reflects light differently from different directions. A "with-nap" cutting layout positions all pattern pieces with the hems pointed in the same direction, which might mean you have to buy more yardage.

ONE-WAY DESIGN LAYOUT When a printed fabric design has a one-way direction, use either a *with-nap layout* or a *one-way design layout*. This keeps all pattern pieces pointed in the same direction.

RIGHT SIDE/WRONG SIDE Every fabric has a "right" side that should face the world—the side with the pattern, the texture, and/or the correct color. The right side/wrong side key on your pattern instruction sheet shows you how to lay out your pattern on the fabric, how to place your pattern pieces, and how to sew the pieces together.

LINING This fabric (usually slippery and silky) is used to finish a garment's interior. Some patterns include separate pattern pieces for the lining; others instruct you to cut the lining with existing pattern pieces. Not all garments are lined.

With-nap layout

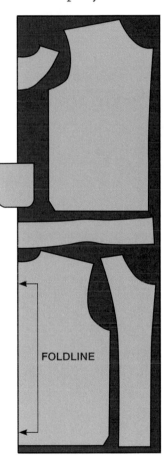

FOLDLINE

CUT ON FOLD For symmetry, pattern pieces are often printed as half pieces, which need to be placed on a folded fabric edge to create a full pattern piece. Simply fold the fabric according to layout directions, then align the marked pattern piece edge with the folded edge.

Facing

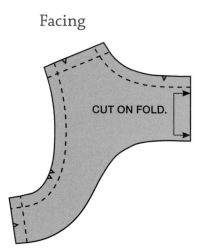

FACING A fabric layer sewn to or folded under to finish an edge. It prevents the edge from stretching, supports the fabric, and, as a separate piece, maintains a curve.

INTERFACING A fabric (usually white or black) used to reinforce, stiffen, or add body to fashion fabric. Fusible varieties have heat-sensitive adhesive on one side. As with lining, some patterns include separate pattern pieces for interfacing, while others instruct you to cut it with existing pattern pieces.

SELVAGE The tightly woven edge on both sides of the fabric.

GRAIN AND GRAINLINE Grain refers to the direction of the yarn in the fabric, which is either lengthwise or crosswise (see p. 108 for more). The long arrow symbol on each pattern piece is placed along the lengthwise grain, which has the straightest and strongest yarns and is parallel to the selvage.

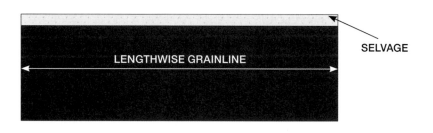

BIAS A true bias lies along an angle 45 degrees to the selvage (see p. 109 for more). In a woven fabric, this direction has the most stretch. When the fabric is cut along this line, the raw edge won't ravel.

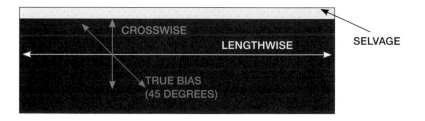

Pattern markings

Every pattern piece includes key wording and symbols to guide you each step of the way.

CUTTING LINE This is the outermost edge of each pattern piece that you cut along. It may be accompanied by a cute scissor icon. For single-size patterns, the cutting line is usually a solid line. For multisize patterns, each line—for each size—has a different dash or dot marking.

FOLDLINE A notation indicating the pattern edge that should be placed on the fabric's fold.

SEAMLINE The line that you sew along, typically ⅝ inch in from the cutting line.

SEAM ALLOWANCE The distance between the cutting line and the seamline. The seam-allowance measurement is noted on the instruction sheet and on the pattern pieces.

NOTCHES Triangles or diamonds printed on the pattern cutting line to help you align seamlines.

ZIPPER END POINT A pattern marking to indicate the bottom edge of a zipper. It is usually marked on the pattern with a circle.

DART LEGS AND POINT Darts are wedges of fabric stitched to shape the garment over curves. The two sides are called legs, and they meet at the point. Darts are marked with lines and dots; align the dots to fold the fabric for stitching.

HEM ALLOWANCE The distance between the cutting line and the hemline. This allowance is folded inside the garment before the hem is sewn. The depth of the hem allowance varies with the garment style and sewing technique (see p. 50 for more).

HEMLINE The lowest edge of the garment once the hem is sewn. It's usually marked with a solid line on the pattern piece.

LENGTHEN/SHORTEN LINES identify where to make length adjustments to the pattern. In most cases, changes made to a front pattern piece should also be made to the corresponding back pattern piece.

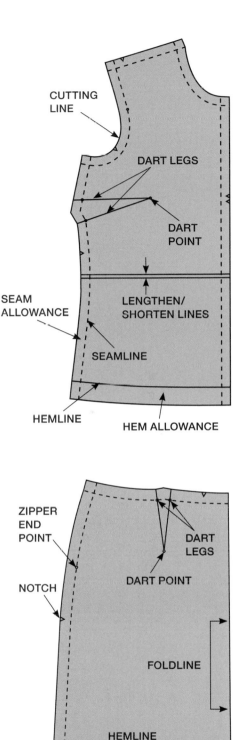

choosing your best pattern size

Selecting the correct pattern size is the first and most important step toward great fit. The process can often be easier than choosing the right size off a ready-to-wear clothing rack: On a pattern envelope you'll find a variety of measurements that will help you to determine the right sizing.

Taking measurements

Grab a measuring tape. Clad in your best-fitting undergarments, measure your circumference at bust level (the fullest part), natural waist (level with your belly button), and hip (7 inches to 9 inches below the waist). Some pattern companies also outline other helpful—but not absolutely necessary—measurements, such as back-waist length and pant inseam. To ensure that you are always prepared, jot down your key measurements and keep them handy in your wallet or file away the info on your smartphone.

Interpreting patterns

Always compare your measurements to those in the pattern-envelope size chart, then select the size that matches yours most closely. If your measurements are ¾ inch or more over a pattern size, go up to the next one. It's easier to take in pattern pieces than to enlarge them.

Interpreting measurements

Women's bodies are a variety of measurement combinations, so don't worry if you don't match up exactly to the envelope's three key measurements. The point is to get as close as possible to a perfect fit, with as few adjustments as possible. Focus on the most important measurement for that particular garment type.

With blouses, jackets, coats, and dresses, the bust is usually the most difficult area to alter—match up that measurement first. With pants and skirts, focus on the larger of your hip and waist measurements. (If, for example, your hip measurement is bigger than your waist, use it to choose a size. If your waist is larger, choose your size based on that.) Once you have chosen a pattern based on the most important measurement, it's only a matter of slight pattern adjustments to get a great fit.

If your measurements don't all match up to a standard pattern size, try multisize patterns, which combine three or more sizes in each pattern piece. You can easily customize the measurements by following the size 10 line in the bust, for example, and then using the size 14 line through the hips.

  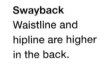  

Correct posture
Waistline and hipline are parallel to the floor.

Body leans back
Waistline and hipline are lower in the back.

Swayback
Waistline and hipline are higher in the back.

Military posture
Center back is shorter, and center front is longer.

Head tilts forward
Center back is longer, and center front is shorter.

Balance

When you're taking your measurements, also take a good look in the mirror—or, better yet, ask a friend to help. Stand up straight, but keep your regular posture, even if you know it's less than perfect. Assess your reflection and compare it to the illustrations above. If the contours of your body don't follow a straight line—and for most of us, they don't—it's something to keep in mind when you get to construction. You may want to adjust the pattern accordingly.

reading
a pattern

So you plunked down some money for a fantastic pattern and have your eye on some pretty fabric. Tap the brakes: This is the time to sit back and read the pattern envelope and instruction sheet carefully, start to finish.

The envelope, please

The information on the front and back of the envelope tells you everything you need to know before you sew a garment: your correct size, how the garment is supposed to fit, and how much fabric to buy.

RECOMMENDED FABRICS (1) For the best results, follow the pattern guidelines. Pay particular attention to suggestions regarding stretch.

BODY MEASUREMENTS (2) These should be old news by now. If you aren't sure what your measurements are, go back and reread the previous section!

YARDAGE REQUIREMENTS (3) Find the requirements for your size in the width of your chosen fabric. Pay attention to notes about purchasing more fabric to match plaids or stripes, and don't forget to look at extras such as lining, interfacing, and trims.

SCHEMATIC DRAWINGS (4) These detailed sketches show every seam, pleat, gather, and closure, and they're a big help in picturing how it will all come together.

FINISHED GARMENT MEASUREMENTS (5) These will help you understand how the sewn garment will fit (see p. 104 for more).

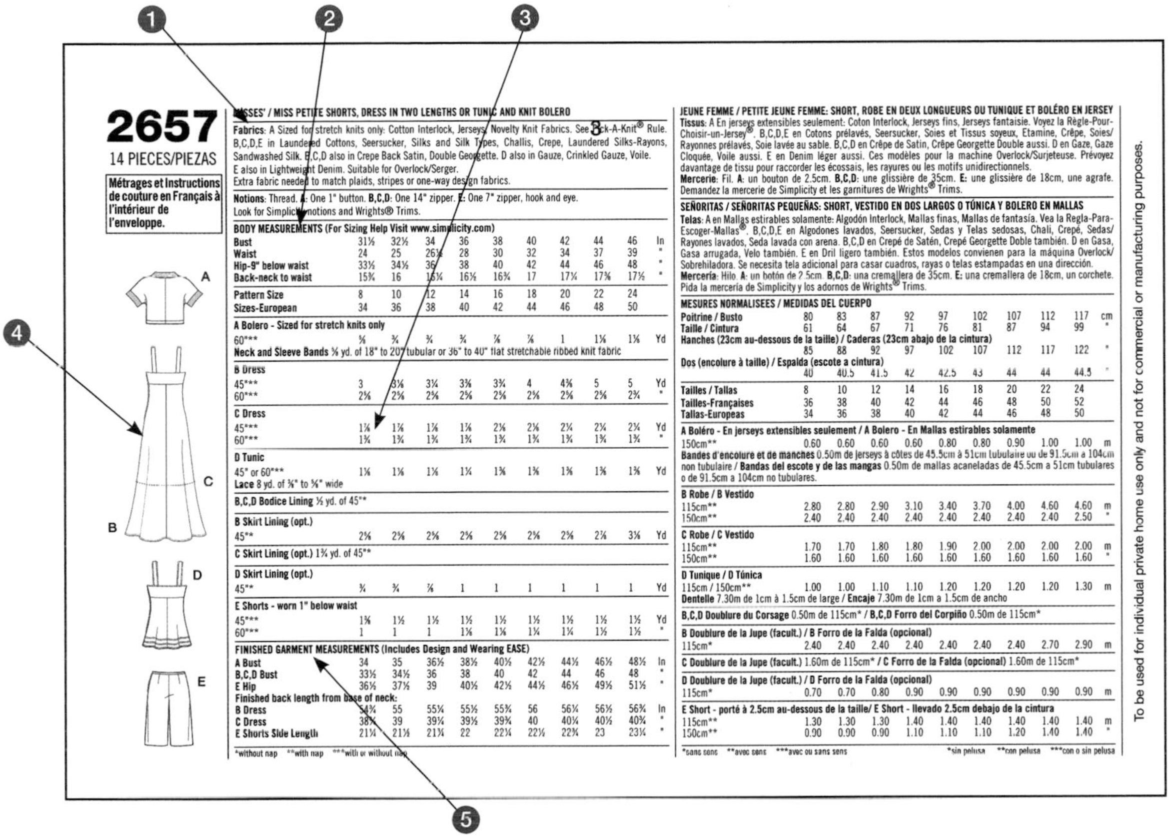

2657

14 PIECES/PIEZAS

Métrages et Instructions de couture en Français à l'intérieur de l'enveloppe.

MISSES' / MISS PETITE SHORTS, DRESS IN TWO LENGTHS OR TUNIC AND KNIT BOLERO

Fabrics: A Sized for stretch knits only: Cotton Interlock, Jerseys, Novelty Knit Fabrics. See Pick-A-Knit® Rule. B,C,D,E in Laundered Cottons, Seersucker, Silks and Silk Types, Challis, Crepe, Laundered Silks-Rayons, Sandwashed Silk. B,C,D also in Crepe Back Satin, Double Georgette. D also in Gauze, Crinkled Gauze, Voile. E also in Lightweight Denim. Suitable for Overlock/Serger. Extra fabric needed to match plaids, stripes or one-way design fabrics.

Notions: Thread. **A**: One 1" button. **B,C,D**: One 14" zipper. **E**: One 7" zipper, hook and eye. Look for Simplicity notions and Wrights® Trims.

BODY MEASUREMENTS (For Sizing Help Visit www.simplicity.com)										
Bust	31½	32½	34	36	38	40	42	44	46	In
Waist	24	25	26½	28	30	32	34	37	39	"
Hip-9" below waist	33½	34½	36	38	40	42	44	46	48	"
Back-neck to waist	15¾	16	16¼	16½	16¾	17	17¼	17⅜	17½	"
Pattern Size	8	10	12	14	16	18	20	22	24	
Sizes-European	34	36	38	40	42	44	46	48	50	
A Bolero - Sized for stretch knits only										
60"***	⅝	¾	¾	¾	⅞	⅞	1	1⅛	1⅛	Yd
Neck and Sleeve Bands ⅜ yd. of 18" to 20" tubular or 36" to 40" flat stretchable ribbed knit fabric										
B Dress										
45"***	3	3⅛	3¼	3⅜	3¾	4	4⅜	5	5	Yd
60"***	2⅝	2⅝	2⅝	2⅝	2⅝	2⅝	2⅝	2⅝	2¾	"
C Dress										
45"***	1⅞	1⅞	1⅞	1⅞	2⅛	2⅛	2¼	2¼	2¼	Yd
60"***	1¾	1¾	1¾	1¾	1¾	1¾	1¾	1¾	1¾	"
D Tunic										
45" or 60"***	1⅛	1⅛	1⅛	1¼	1⅜	1⅜	1⅜	1⅜	1⅜	Yd
Lace 8 yd. of ⅜" to ⅝" wide										
B,C,D Bodice Lining ½ yd. of 45"*										
B Skirt Lining (opt.)										
45"*	2⅝	2⅝	2⅝	2⅝	2⅝	2⅝	2⅝	2⅞	3⅛	Yd
C Skirt Lining (opt.) 1¾ yd. of 45"*										
D Skirt Lining (opt.)										
45"*	¾	¾	⅞	1	1	1	1	1	1	Yd
E Shorts - worn 1" below waist										
45"***	1⅜	1½	1½	1½	1½	1½	1½	1½	1½	Yd
60"***	1	1	1	1⅛	1⅛	1¼	1¼	1½	1½	"
FINISHED GARMENT MEASUREMENTS (Includes Design and Wearing EASE)										
A Bust	34	35	36½	38½	40½	42½	44½	46½	48½	In
B,C,D Bust	33½	34½	36	38	40	42	44	46	48	"
E Hip	36½	37½	39	40½	42½	44½	46½	49½	51½	"
Finished back length from base of neck:										
B Dress	54¾	55	55¼	55½	55¾	56	56¼	56½	56¾	In
C Dress	38¾	39	39¼	39½	39¾	40	40¼	40½	40¾	"
E Shorts Side Length	21¼	21½	21¾	22	22¼	22½	22¾	23	23¼	"

*without nap **with nap ***with or without nap

JEUNE FEMME / PETITE JEUNE FEMME: SHORT, ROBE EN DEUX LONGUEURS OU TUNIQUE ET BOLÉRO EN JERSEY

Tissus: A En jerseys extensibles seulement: Coton Interlock, Jerseys fins, Jerseys fantaisie. Voyez la Règle-Pour-Choisir-un-Jersey®. B,C,D,E en Cotons prélavés, Seersucker, Soies et Tissus soyeux, Etamine, Crêpe, Soies/Rayonnes prélavés, Soie lavée au sable. B,C,D en Crêpe de Satin, Crêpe Georgette Double aussi. D en Gaze, Gaze Cloquée, Voile aussi. E en Denim léger aussi. Ces modèles pour la machine Overlock/Surjeteuse. Prévoyez davantage de tissu pour raccorder les écossais, les rayures ou les motifs unidirectionnels.

Mercerie: Fil. **A**: un bouton de 2.5cm. **B,C,D**: une glissière de 35cm. **E**: une glissière de 18cm, une agrafe. Demandez la mercerie de Simplicity et les garnitures de Wrights® Trims.

SEÑORITAS / SEÑORITAS PEQUEÑAS: SHORT, VESTIDO EN DOS LARGOS O TÚNICA Y BOLERO EN MALLAS

Telas: A en Mallas estirables solamente: Algodón Interlock, Mallas finas, Mallas de fantasía. Vea la Regla-Para-Escoger-Mallas®. B,C,D,E en Algodones lavados, Seersucker, Sedas y Telas sedosas, Chali, Crepé, Sedas/Rayones lavados, Seda lavada con arena. B,C,D en Crepé de Satén, Crepé Georgette Doble también. D en Gasa, Gasa arrugada, Velo también. E en Dril ligero también. Estos modelos convienen para la máquina Overlock/Sobrehiladora. Se necesita tela adicional para casar cuadros, rayas o telas estampadas en una dirección.

Mercería: Hilo. **A**: un botón de 2.5cm. **B,C,D**: una cremallera de 35cm. **E**: una cremallera de 18cm, un corchete. Pida la mercería de Simplicity y los adornos de Wrights® Trims.

MESURES NORMALISEES / MEDIDAS DEL CUERPO										
Poitrine / Busto	80	83	87	92	97	102	107	112	117	cm
Taille / Cintura	61	64	67	71	76	81	87	94	99	"
Hanches (23cm au-dessous de la taille) / Caderas (23cm abajo de la cintura)	85	88	92	97	102	107	112	117	122	"
Dos (encolure à taille) / Espalda (escote a cintura)	40	40.5	41.5	42	42.5	43	44	44	44.5	"
Tailles / Tallas	8	10	12	14	16	18	20	22	24	
Tailles-Françaises	36	38	40	42	44	46	48	50	52	
Tallas-Europeas	34	36	38	40	42	44	46	48	50	
A Boléro - En jerseys extensibles seulement / A Bolero - En Mallas estirables solamente										
150cm**	0.60	0.60	0.60	0.60	0.80	0.80	0.90	1.00	1.00	m
Bandes d'encolure et de manches 0.50m de jerseys à côtes de 45.5cm à 51cm tubulaire ou de 91.5cm à 104cm non tubulaire / **Bandas del escote y de las mangas** 0.50m de mallas acaneladas de 45.5cm a 51cm tubulares o de 91.5cm a 104cm no tubulares.										
B Robe / B Vestido										
115cm**	2.80	2.80	2.90	3.10	3.40	3.70	4.00	4.60	4.60	m
150cm**	2.40	2.40	2.40	2.40	2.40	2.40	2.40	2.40	2.50	"
C Robe / C Vestido										
115cm**	1.70	1.70	1.80	1.80	1.90	2.00	2.00	2.00	2.00	m
150cm**	1.60	1.60	1.60	1.60	1.60	1.60	1.60	1.60	1.60	"
D Tunique / D Túnica										
115cm / 150cm**	1.00	1.00	1.10	1.10	1.20	1.20	1.20	1.20	1.30	m
Dentelle 7.30m de 1cm à 1.5cm de large / **Encaje** 7.30m de 1cm a 1.5cm de ancho										
B,C,D Doublure du Corsage 0.50m de 115cm* / **B,C,D Forro del Corpiño** 0.50m de 115cm*										
B Doublure de la Jupe (facult.) / B Forro de la Falda (opcional)										
115cm*	2.40	2.40	2.40	2.40	2.40	2.40	2.40	2.70	2.90	m
C Doublure de la Jupe (facult.) 1.60m de 115cm* / **C Forro de la Falda (opcional)** 1.60m de 115cm*										
D Doublure de la Jupe (facult.) / D Forro de la Falda (opcional)										
115cm*	0.70	0.70	0.80	0.90	0.90	0.90	0.90	0.90	0.90	m
E Short - porté à 2.5cm au-dessous de la taille/ E Short - llevado 2.5cm debajo de la cintura										
115cm**	1.30	1.30	1.30	1.40	1.40	1.40	1.40	1.40	1.40	m
150cm**	0.90	0.90	0.90	1.10	1.10	1.10	1.20	1.40	1.40	"

*sans sens **avec sens ***avec ou sans sens *sin pelusa **con pelusa ***con o sin pelusa

To be used for individual private home use only and not for commercial or manufacturing purposes.

make it simple

Technology can be your sewing ally. You can scan or take digital photos of the front and back of pattern envelopes, then sort them into electronic folders in your computer. You can even print out these files to display many patterns on a single sheet of paper. Paste the thumbnail sheet on the front of your storage box to indicate its contents.

Guide sheets

Pattern guide sheets are enormously helpful, even for veteran sewers. Be sure to look over the instructions before you begin.

PATTERN PIECES (1) Use these outline drawings and the list that follows to identify the pieces you need for the garment.

GENERAL DIRECTIONS (2) Read through the directions to interpret symbols and terms on the guide sheet and pattern tissue.

LAYOUT DIAGRAMS (3) Follow these diagrams to cut the garment from the amount of fabric listed on the envelope. If you have less fabric than recommended, a creative layout could accommodate the pattern pieces.

SEWING DIRECTIONS (4) Read the how-to all the way through before starting. If several views share steps, you can easily get sidetracked. If there are any potentially confusing parts, highlight the steps you need.

Reading a pattern and its envelope can shed new light on how to create clothes you love to make and to wear.

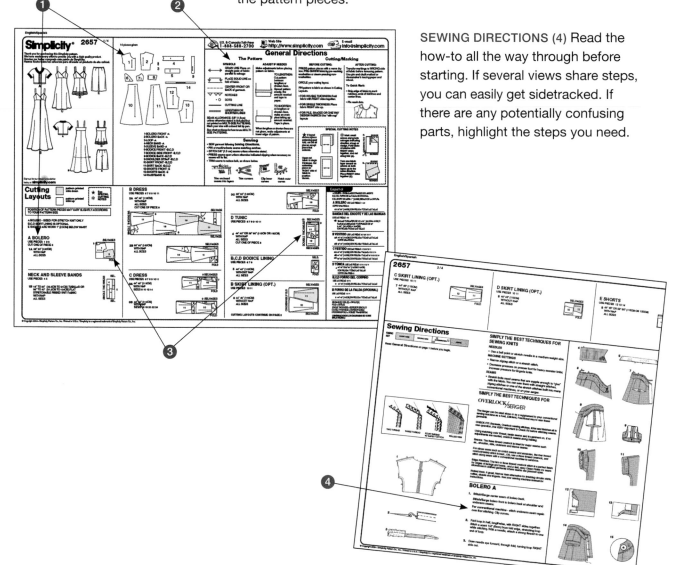

Pattern tissue

Cut each pattern piece on the appropriate line for your size. Look over each piece before you lay it on the fabric to identify the symbols that apply to the view you're making.

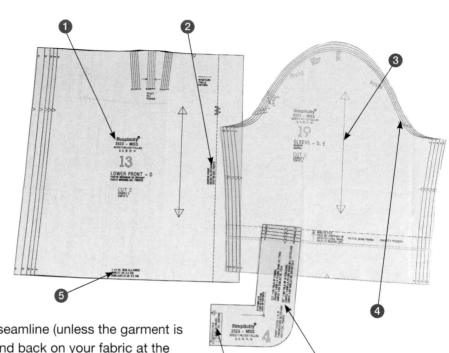

PATTERN ID (1) The pattern company name, pattern number, size, and the number of the pattern piece all help you keep track of the pieces you're using.

CENTERS FRONT AND BACK (2) These crucial landmarks are typically positioned along a fold or seamline (unless the garment is asymmetrical). Mark centers front and back on your fabric at the edges with clips or notches so you can refer to them throughout construction.

GRAINLINE (3) Position the grainline parallel to the fabric selvage. If the printed grainline is short, extend it to both ends of the pattern piece. Before laying out a pattern, double-check that the selvage is perpendicular to the crosswise grain.

NOTCHES, DOTS, CIRCLES, SQUARES (4) These symbols provide landmarks for construction steps. Mark them so they're easy to locate when you're sewing.

HEMLINES AND FOLDLINES (5) Note that the hemline is labeled with the expected hem allowance for the design. You can adjust that to suit your project. Vertical foldlines, such as those at a center-front opening, should be marked with clips at each end or a chalkline.

CUTTING AND PLACE-ON-A-FOLD LINES (6) Most patterns are multisize, so there are several cutting lines on each piece. Highlight your size before cutting to avoid veering off course. Be sure to lay pattern pieces marked "place on a fold" on the fabric fold.

WRITTEN INSTRUCTIONS (7) These instructions tell you what to do with each pattern piece.

ease: it's easy

When you try clothes and look in the mirror, ease—the difference between your actual body measurement and the finished measurement of what you're wearing—is probably not the first thing that comes to mind. But the amount of ease included in a garment directly affects its fit, appearance, and comfort.

Types of ease

Wearing ease—typically 2 inches to 3 inches added to the bust, waist, hip, and other key points—is built into most basic patterns. It allows you to breathe and move in your clothes and to sit comfortably in pants or a skirt. **Design ease** is added to the basic pattern (above and beyond wearing ease) for specific fit or activity. A comfy pajama top, for example, has much more ease

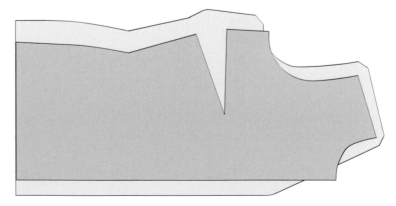

This pink pattern has almost no ease. The blue pattern underneath it is for the same size body, but it has enough ease added for a fitted garment.

than a tailored jacket. Design ease also takes layering needs into consideration.

The two pattern pieces shown on the facing page show how ease works. The smaller pattern has minimum ease built in. It is drafted based on the body measurements from the shoulders to the hips. The larger pattern has ease added. The armhole is lower, the shoulder is wider, and the pattern is wider at the side seams for comfort, and at the center where the front overlaps for buttons. The neckline is also a different shape. All of this added space makes the garment wearable.

Determining ease

If you figure out how much ease you want your garments to have, you will save hours struggling to make a pattern fit the way you'd like it to. Here's how to do it: Measure the bust and hip of your favorite jacket and compare to your own measurements. The difference between the jacket and your body measurements is the amount of ease included in the jacket. Do this for a variety of garments, and take notes on what you like best—say, flowy tops and snug skirts.

Next, compare the pattern company's size chart to the finished garment measurement chart. For example, if the pattern company's size 12 has a bust measurement of 34 inches, and the finished garment measurement is 40 inches, there are 6 inches of ease in the pattern. Compare your preferences to ease amounts in different patterns so you can pick those that need minimal alterations and will give you a flattering, comfortable fit.

The pattern description also often clues you in to the amount of ease, with the terms close-fitting, fitted, semifitted, loose fitting, or very loose fitting. The ease built into a garment can range from no ease or even negative ease (stretches to fit your body) for a close-fitting garment to 12 inches or more for a very loose fitting garment.

The difference between your body measurements and a finished garment is the garment's ease.

Standard ease amounts

TIGHT FITTING

Bust—minus 2 inches to 4 inches for dresses and tops

Hips—minus 2 inches to 4 inches for skirts, pants, and shorts

CLOSE FITTING

Bust—1 inch to 2⅞ inches for dresses, blouses, and tops

Hips—1 inch to 1⅞ inches for skirts, pants, shorts, and culottes

FITTED

Bust—3 inches to 4 inches for dresses, blouses, tops, and vests; 3¾ inches to 4¼ inches for jackets; and 5¼ inches to 6¾ inches for coats

Hips—2 inches to 3 inches for skirts, pants, shorts, and culottes

TIGHT FITTING These are the clothes a dancer, gymnast, or skater wears. They are always made of fabrics that stretch in both directions. Because they are intended to be very snug, they are sewn with negative ease. When held up to your body these garments are much smaller, but they stretch to fit.

CLOSE FITTING Jeans are the perfect example of a close-fitting garment: they have to have some ease or you couldn't get into them. This is not a good fit for clothes made of lightweight sheer fabrics.

FITTED This can range from a strapless gown to a body-hugging suit or coat. A fitted garment should be made of a fabric that has stability and an adequate weight. If it's a gown, it may have underlayers to support sheer layers. This garment is likely to involve tailoring techniques to make and preserve the fitted shape.

SEMIFITTED

Bust—$4\frac{1}{8}$ inches to 5 inches for dresses, blouses, tops, and vests; $4\frac{3}{8}$ inches to $5\frac{3}{4}$ inches for jackets; and $6\frac{7}{8}$ inches to 8 inches for coats

Hips—$3\frac{1}{8}$ inches to 4 inches for skirts, pants, shorts, and culottes

LOOSE FITTING

Bust—$5\frac{1}{8}$ inches to 8 inches for dresses, blouses, tops, and vests; $5\frac{7}{8}$ inches to 10 inches for jackets; and $8\frac{1}{8}$ inches to 12 inches for coats

Hips—$4\frac{1}{8}$ inches to 6 inches for skirts, pants, shorts, and culottes

VERY LOOSE FITTING

Bust—More than 8 inches for dresses, blouses, tops, and vests; more than 10 inches for jackets; and more than 12 inches for coats

Hips—More than 6 inches for skirts, pants, shorts, and culottes

SEMIFITTED Most suits and coats that have a fitted nature will fall into this category rather than the fitted category if they are worn over other clothes. They have shaping, darts, and curved seams and show the figure without hugging it too closely. This fit is good for knits, wovens, and a variety of weights suitable for all seasons.

LOOSE FITTING Relaxed and sporty, this fit and style can also be luxurious. This is where you'll see some of the fantasy fabrics like brocade and satin or velvet, because they don't have to be forced into strenuous fitting. But it's equally comfortable for linen, cotton, suit-weight, and shirt-weight fabrics.

VERY LOOSE FITTING This fit often has an artsy look—think palazzo pants and caftans. It is a delicious match for fabulous fabrics. You can also try chiffon and gauze, and let the garment volume make up for the weightlessness of the fabric. Alternatively, you can capitalize on the volume with a punchy fabric, such as taffeta in a bright color, and make a statement.

getting your grain

All woven fabrics have what's called grain. There is straight grain, cross-grain, and bias. These grains determine whether a fabric is stiff, stretchy, or super easy to drape. Pattern manufacturers clearly mark the straight grain on every pattern piece with a long arrow to indicate where you have to place each one. If you don't understand grain and you place your pattern piece incorrectly, you're going to run into problems. But don't fret! It's simpler than it sounds.

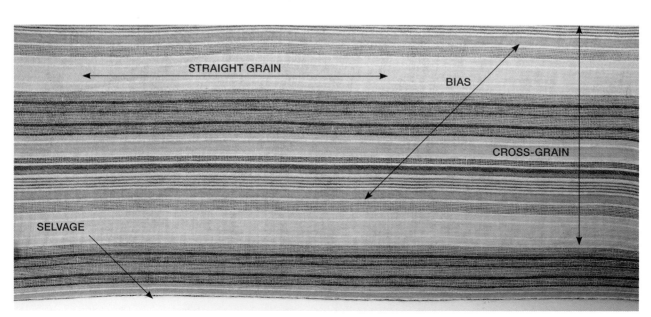

STRAIGHT GRAIN

BIAS

CROSS-GRAIN

SELVAGE

The stripes on these samples run with the straight grain.

Which way is your fabric going?

Each grain runs in a different direction on the cloth.

STRAIGHT GRAIN When fabric is woven, the yarn is stretched tight and straight on a loom. This is known as the **warp** or **straight grain**. The warp threads run parallel to the selvage. Most woven fabrics have little or no stretch on the straight grain—even fabric blends containing stretchy fibers, like spandex. Garments are usually cut with the straight grain running vertically along the garment. The center front and center back lines on a garment are generally placed on the exact straight grain of the fabric. This gives the garment vertical stability and keeps it from stretching in the length, so hemlines stay even.

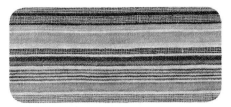

STRAIGHT GRAIN

CROSS-GRAIN Threads or yarn that run perpendicular to the straight grain are called the **cross-grain** or **weft**. In the most basic weave, the weft alternates running over and under the warp threads. By using different colors and methods, a design can be woven into the cloth, such as on twills, damask, or brocade. In the fabric shown at right, the weft yarns are a neutral color and nearly disappear into the striped warp yarns. When fabrics have an iridescent quality or look like two distinct colors from different directions, the warp yarns are one color and the weft another. Unlike straight-grain yarns, cross-grain threads aren't constantly pulled tight, so they have some give. The fabric's cross-grain is typically placed on the circumference of a garment. This works perfectly for areas that require a little flexibility, like the hip and waist.

CROSS-GRAIN

BIAS The bias is a product of the straight grain and cross-grain when you cut through them at an angle. When the angle is 45 degrees to the straight or cross-grain, it's called the **true bias**. A true bias grain has wonderful properties, but because it involves placing the pattern pieces on the fabric diagonally, a bias layout usually requires more fabric than a standard straight-grain layout. The true bias has considerably more stretch than the other two grains. When you stretch fabric along the bias in one direction, the other direction gets narrower. This stretchy property usually hides in the fabric until you cut it into pattern-size pieces.

BIAS

Properly placing your pattern piece on the fabric with respect to the grain is essential to successful sewing.

But it can also quietly do its work without you even noticing. For example, a section of the curve in an armhole is cut on the bias, which helps the active seam fit better and be more comfortable because of the natural stretch. Another bonus? A raw bias-cut edge doesn't ravel, so you don't have to finish it. All sewers depend on bias-cut strips of fabric to make perfect bindings because they fold around a curved edge without puckering. Whole garments cut on the bias are known for their elegant drape, easy unconstructed fit, and beautiful lines.

Fabric pulled with the grain has little stretch. Pulled cross-grain, it has slight stretch.

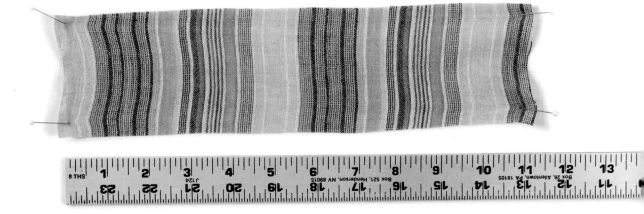

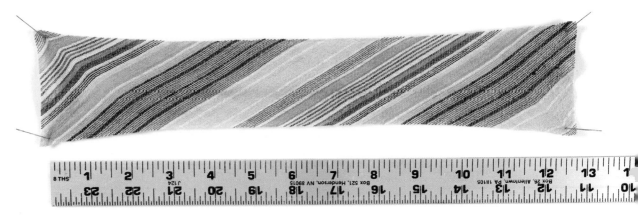

When bias is stretched in one direction it gets longer, but the opposite direction gets narrower. These photos show the same strip stretched in opposite directions. Compare the results to their measurements.

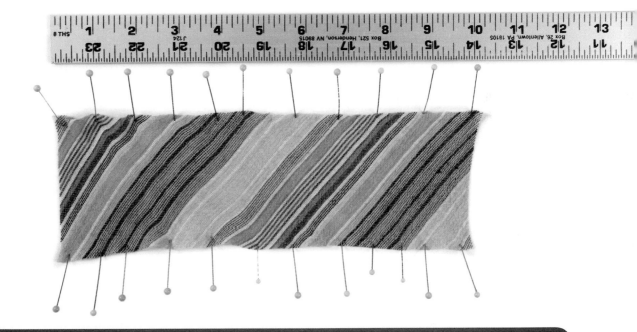

make it simple

Here's a simple trick for placing pattern pieces (even irregular ones, like pants or facings) on grain using a piece of lined notebook paper, two pins, and a straightedge. Position one of the lines on the paper over the grainline on the pattern piece. Then, find one of the outer lines on the notebook paper that is at or outside the widest part of the pattern piece. Highlight that line and use it to align your grainline. With this trick, you establish a grainline to refer to, and eliminate unnecessary measuring, pinning, and unpinning.

pinning

For many sewers, the good old pin is the tool of choice. A few well-placed pins stabilize and control any type of fabric, which results in precise cutting and accurate, frustration-free sewing. The key to cutting accurately is to lay out the fabric on a flat surface, smooth it out to remove all wrinkles, and make sure the grainlines are straight. Then pin carefully without disturbing the fabric.

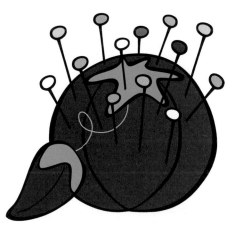

How to pin
Follow these instructions for correct pinning.

PLACE PINS PARALLEL TO SEAMLINES Parallel pinning doesn't disturb the fabric and ensures that the pins will never wander out past the cutting line. You can damage your scissors if you accidentally snip a pin that's placed perpendicular to the seamline.

USE AS FEW PINS AS POSSIBLE Even the sharpest, finest pin creates a tiny hole in your fabric, so space your pins about 3 inches apart.

DO NOT LIFT THE FABRIC Place the palm of your free hand on the fabric to keep it flat on the table, and use your index finger to guide the pins up through the fabric.

Places to pin

The general rule for pinning is to use as few as possible, but there are three areas that require a little extra attention.

CURVES Necklines, armholes, curved hems, and crotch curves need extra pins to secure the fabric.

CORNERS Place the head of a pin at the corner, and face the point in toward the garment. Make sure the pin does not cross the cutting line.

FOLDLINES To ensure that pattern pieces placed along the fold of the fabric don't shift, place pins every 3 inches along the fold.

Pin to sew

When you pin fabric pieces together to sew, the goal is to secure and control the fabric as well as to position the pins so that you can easily remove them before they go under the presser foot. Never sew over a pin: Hitting one can damage the pin or the machine's needle.

Place pins perpendicular to seamlines. Align them with their heads facing to the right of your machine's presser foot. To evenly distribute the fabric, place a pin at both ends of the seam, then at the notch or other halfway mark; continue to place pins halfway between the existing pins until the fabric is secured. A pin every 2 inches to 3 inches is a good rule, but you might need more for slippery fabrics.

Dull, bent, or rusted pins can wreak havoc on your fabric. Discard them.

make it simple

When pinning a long seam that needs to have a space left open (for example, when stitching a pillow that will be turned right side out), use a two-pin system to remind yourself to stop. Pin in the normal fashion, but when you get to the location where the stitching should stop, place two pins close together. Use double pins to mark the location where you should start stitching again. As soon as you see the first set of two pins, you immediately know to stop stitching. Use this technique for marking zipper insertion stops, large dots, or any other location where the stitching needs to end.

working with a dress form

A dress form—that headless, linen-covered figure that's synonymous with the dressmaker's craft—isn't usually the first tool a novice sewer purchases, but you can definitely benefit from having one around. Your new buddy will always reveal the truth about a garment's fit, proportions, and construction, and can help you fix any problems you uncover.

Why you need a dress form

No matter how simple the garment, you'll understand its structure and fit better when you can see it on a three-dimensional human shape. If you want to make changes to a commercial pattern or draft your own, a dress form allows you to verify that it will translate into the garment you've envisioned. And if you're interested in draping garments from scratch, a dress form is essential equipment.

Fitting a dress form to your figure

A dress form is most helpful when it's an exact duplicate of your figure, but few of us resemble the standardized shapes of commercial forms. Any dress form can be customized by adding some padding—some are even sold with pads and batting for this purpose. Others have dials that increase or decrease the height and girth of the form. Most tops, dresses, coats, and jackets hang from the shoulders, so this is the area to fit most accurately. For example, if your shoulders are narrow but your bust is full, purchase a form that matches your shoulder width and pad the bust to size.

Dress form features

Your sewing habits will dictate the type of form that's best for you. Decide which features you need.

PINNABLE (1) You'll be fitting garments on the form, so it's important that you can pin directly onto the form to hold fabric and pattern pieces in position.

BIFURCATED (2) If you need to fit pants, look for a form with shaped thighs and seat.

HEM FRIENDLY (3) A hem gauge and height markings on the center pole enable you to establish even hems.

STURDILY MOUNTED (4) The heavier the base, the heavier the garment it can support without toppling. Casters are helpful if you move your form around.

COLLAPSIBLE (5) Professional-type dress forms often feature collapsible shoulders to facilitate dressing and undressing the form.

ADJUSTABLE (6) If you plan to use your form to represent several different people, an easily adjustable one can save you time and money.

ROTATING (7) A form that turns on its supporting pole (smoothly but not too quickly) makes easy work of fitting garments from all angles.

STEAMABLE If you sew traditionally tailored garments, you may want to steam garment sections into shape directly on the form. If so, choose a composition that can handle the heat and humidity.

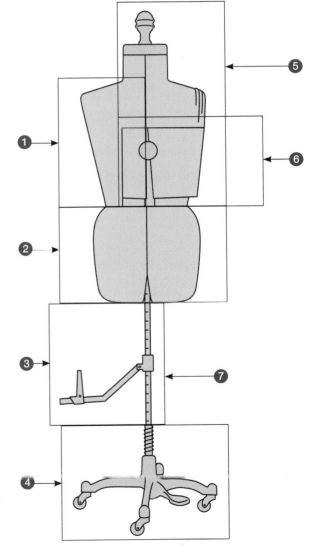

laying out: when you want to do it your way

Pattern instructions are great . . . except when they're not. Some patterns have limited or confusing directions, instead of a step-by-step how-to. A few might be missing them entirely. And for patterns written in a different language, you might have trouble understanding the translation—or there might not be one. Lack of specific sewing instructions isn't a cause for panic, though. If your best friend nabbed you a gorgeous kimono pattern when she was in Tokyo, you don't have to learn the Hiragana syllabary. There are general assembly guidelines that apply to every garment. All you need to do is focus on one garment piece, or section, at a time.

Sewing in sections

The logical sequence of assembly in purchased patterns is sometimes compromised in an effort to streamline the steps. For example, topstitching may not be the last step, but it might be listed at the end to save space. Sewing section by section, in comparison, is always logical and easy to follow. It also helps with time management because you can check off your progress in small increments.

Planning

Just because you're working without step-by-step directions doesn't mean you shouldn't have a plan of attack. Spend time creating a map similar to the sketched sequences shown on pp. 117–119. Collect all necessary supplies, prewash your fabric, cut out your pieces, and identify the right side on each (a small safety pin works well for this). Mark matching points, interface as needed, and you're ready to sew.

Finishing touches

Once all the sections are joined and the garment has taken shape, just add the last lines of topstitching and hand stitching as needed, hem the garment, and add closures. Then step back and admire your work.

Building your garment section by section

1. **Get the small pieces ready.** Prepare or construct small garment pieces or details (pockets, waistbands, facing sections, collars, and cuffs), then set them aside.

2. **Complete each section in its entirety.** Next, choose a section, such as a pant front. Start on the inside, move out to the edges, then layer small pieces or details on top. For example, sew interior darts, staystitch, then attach a patch pocket.

3. **Join all the sections together.** When all sections are completed, simply sew them together. Below and on pp. 118–119 you'll find a basic sequence for a skirt, blouse, and pants.

SKIRT

1. Get the small pieces ready.

Interface   Interface   Interface   Press the
                                                edge up and
                                                topstitch.

BACK   FRONT   BACK   FACING

2. Complete each section in its entirety.

×2   Sew the dart.

                  Topstitch.

CENTER   SIDE   FRONT   CENTER   ZIPPER   BACK
FRONT   FRONT   BACK
                                             ×2
                                    BACK

3. Join all the sections together.

                                                          Topstitch.

FRONT   BACK   FACING   Hem

BLOUSE

1. Get the small pieces ready.

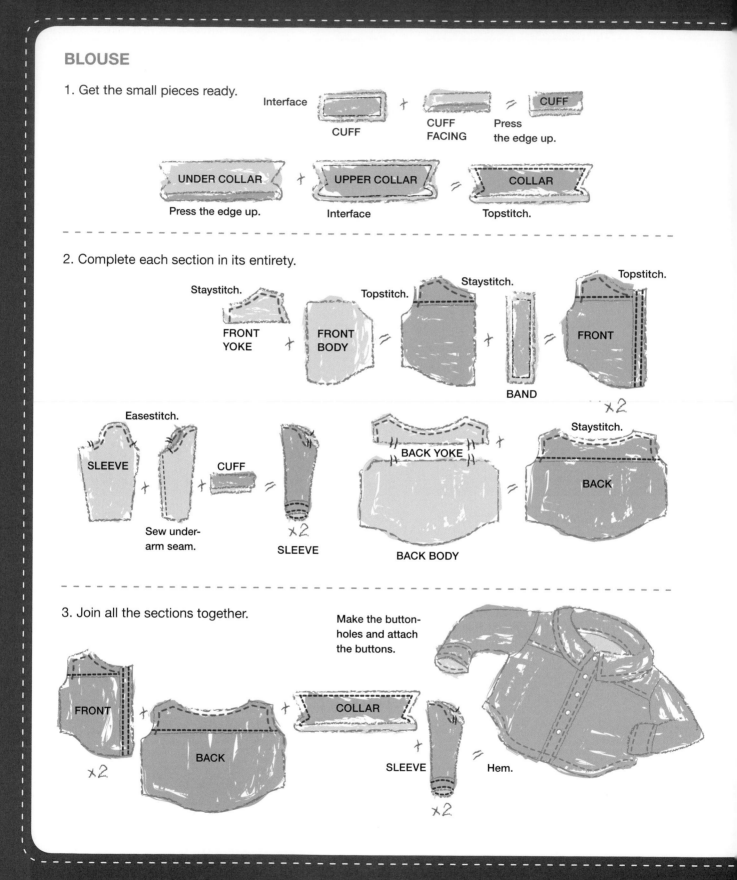

Interface

CUFF + CUFF FACING = CUFF Press the edge up.

UNDER COLLAR + UPPER COLLAR = COLLAR

Press the edge up. Interface Topstitch.

2. Complete each section in its entirety.

Staystitch. Topstitch. Staystitch. Topstitch.

FRONT YOKE + FRONT BODY = + BAND = FRONT

×2

Easestitch. Staystitch.

SLEEVE + + CUFF = BACK YOKE + BACK

Sew under-arm seam. SLEEVE ×2 BACK BODY

3. Join all the sections together.

Make the button-holes and attach the buttons.

FRONT + BACK + COLLAR + SLEEVE = Hem.

×2 ×2

PANTS

1. Get the small pieces ready.

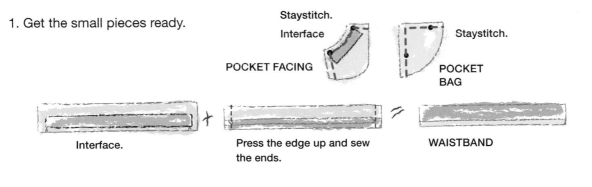

Staystitch.
Interface
POCKET FACING

Staystitch.
POCKET BAG

Interface.

Press the edge up and sew the ends.

WAISTBAND

2. Complete each section in its entirety.

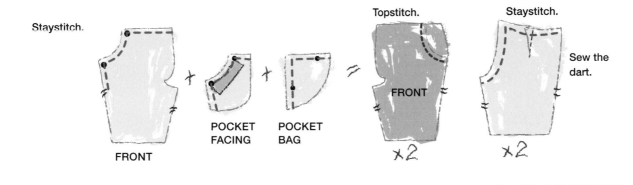

Staystitch.

FRONT

POCKET FACING

POCKET BAG

Topstitch.

FRONT

×2

Staystitch.

Sew the dart.

×2

3. Join all the sections together.

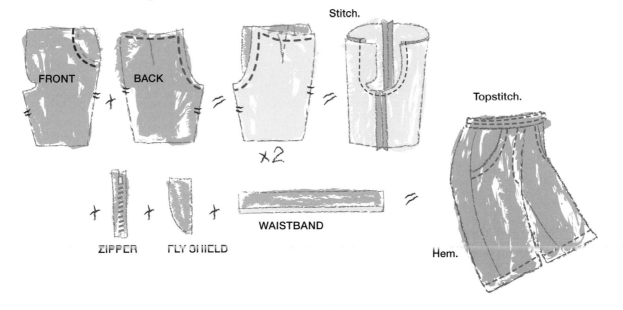

FRONT

BACK

×2

Stitch.

Topstitch.

ZIPPER

FLY SHIELD

WAISTBAND

Hem.

4

patterned projects

Now that you're an expert on patterns, you can put together a garment with confidence and ease. When using any pattern, including the ones in this chapter, experiment and remember that you can change it around to suit your tastes.

------------------------------ ✼ ------------------------------

This chapter, like Chapter 2, is divided into three sections: "Good to Start With," "When You're Getting Comfortable," and "If You're Feeling Inspired." You can work your way from the simpler projects to the more challenging ones, or just jump into the first one that catches your eye. If you've already worked on the pattern-free projects in this book, you're familiar with "The Usual Suspects." This is a list of basic sewing supplies that you'll need for pretty much everything you ever sew. In each project we list The Usual Suspects, followed by the amount of fabric you'll need, plus any extra supplies

the usual suspects

- ❏ Fabric
- ❏ Matching thread
- ❏ Measuring tools (ruler, measuring tape, seam gauge, yardstick, French curve)
- ❏ Cutting tools (shears, scissors, rotary cutter and mat, seam ripper)
- ❏ Needles and pins (thimble, pincushion, beeswax)
- ❏ Iron

silk scarf

what you'll need

The Usual Suspects (see p. 121)

2 yards 44-inch-wide silk charmeuse

Silk thread

Seed beads

Get acquainted with silk charmeuse by making a simple, elegant scarf with seed-bead stripes. Two yards of charmeuse yield a luxurious scarf, approximately 21 inches by 70 inches. All seam allowances are ½ inch.

1 Following the pattern diagrams at right, draft each pattern piece on paper and cut the scarf sections. With right sides together, sew one long edge of the rectangles together. Press the seam allowances as sewn, then open.

2 Hand-sew seed beads across the scarf's short ends. A machine-stitched zigzag is a great guide for placing the beads. Sew on the beads from about ½ inch outside the seam allowance (to be free of the presser foot when you sew the other long seam), across the scarf end and the seam, and to ½ inch outside the opposite seam allowance (see photo below).

3 With right sides together, sew around the remaining three edges. Leave an opening for turning. Complete the beading rows. Turn the scarf right side out, steam-press it, then slipstitch the opening closed.

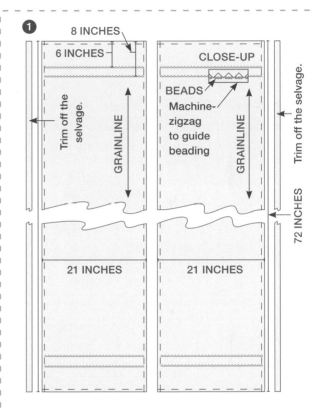

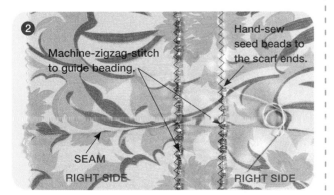

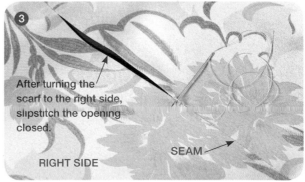

grecian tank

what you'll need

The Usual Suspects (see p. 121)

1 yard to 2 yards summer-weight fabric (depending on the desired length)

This little tank-style dress, meant to be worn as a summer cover-up, is based on a basic T-shirt pattern. Add length and width to the pattern to suit your own body type and style preferences. The garment has fashionably deep armholes and statement-making shoulder loops. A light-colored cotton and Lycra blend will keep its shape *and* keep you cool.

1 Lengthen the T-shirt pattern into a tunic. Measure from your upper shoulder point to the desired tunic length. Extend the T-shirt pattern to the new length, plus hem allowance. For this style, we added 14 inches at the hem.

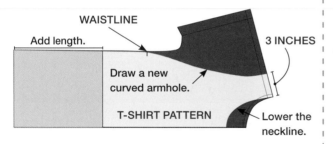

WAISTLINE

Add length.

3 INCHES

Draw a new curved armhole.

T-SHIRT PATTERN

Lower the neckline.

2 Add width to the body. On the pattern front, draw two lines from a point in the underarm to the hem. Angle the lines to be a few inches apart at the hem. Cut along the lines and spread the pattern pieces apart. Determine the total extra width you wish to add to the garment. Each slash represents one-eighth of the added width. (Both the front and back have four slashes.) For the design shown, we added a total of 4 inches, ½ inch in each slash.

3 Lower the front neckline. Use a fashion ruler to draft the curve. Be sure the line crosses the center front at a 90-degree angle for a smooth curve. For the design shown, we lowered the neckline 3 inches.

4 Draft a strap and armhole. **Mark the strap width 3 inches from the neck edge on the** shoulder seam. Mark the pattern waistline on the side seam. Use a fashion ruler as a guide to draw a curved armhole between the marks. Make sure the line meets the shoulder at a 90-degree angle.

5 Sew the side seams, with right sides together. **Do not sew the shoulder seams.** Use a 4 mm-wide double needle to topstitch the garment's raw edges. Fold under ⅜ inch on the armholes and neckline, and 1 inch for the hem.

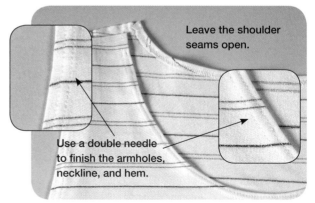

Leave the shoulder seams open.

Use a double needle to finish the armholes, neckline, and hem.

6 Cut strips for the strap-top loops. **Cut a fabric strip 2¾ inches by 3¾ inches.** Fold the fabric strip lengthwise with right sides together. Sew the long edge, leaving ⅜ inch unsewn at each end.

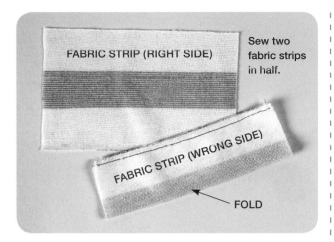

FABRIC STRIP (RIGHT SIDE)

Sew two fabric strips in half.

FABRIC STRIP (WRONG SIDE)

FOLD

7 Turn the strip right side out. **Form it into a loop by placing one short edge within the other. Fold the seam allowances in and hand-stitch the opening closed.**

8 Slide the fabric loops onto the garment's front straps. Push them down a few inches. Pin and sew the shoulder seam, with right sides together. Then slide the loops up to cover the seam. Hand-tack the loops in place.

Slide the loops onto the straps.

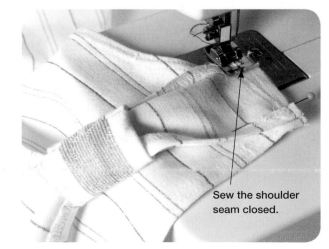

Sew the shoulder seam closed.

wrap dress

what you'll need

The Usual Suspects (see p. 121)

2¾ yards jersey fabric

Gridded pattern paper

Hooks and eyes,
three small flat sets

2½-inch-wide novelty belt buckle

Serger (optional)

Pattern on p. 129

Customize this versatile wrap dress with fabrics, leather belt pieces, or a vintage belt buckle. For example, you can transform this uptown look to boho chic by choosing a paisley fabric and extending the hemline to ankle length. No matter what look you're going for, select a high-quality jersey with some Lycra content in a fine-gauge knit. Leaving some edges raw lets this dress drape and flow in a flattering way, so you want a jersey that will not ravel or curl excessively along a cut edge. Ask for swatches to test before you buy.

---

1 **Draft the pieces.** Following the pattern diagrams (p. 129), draft each pattern piece on paper in the desired size. Transfer all markings.

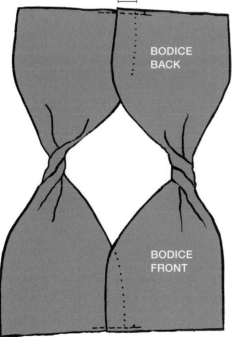

1½ INCHES

BODICE
BACK

BODICE
FRONT

1½ INCHES

Overlap the right and left bodice pieces at the center back. Twist the right and left bodice pieces for the shoulder effect, overlap them at the center front, and secure.

2 **Cut the fabric.** Cut two bodice pieces, two skirt pieces, and six belt pieces. (You'll use two belt pieces to create the back belt, and four belt pieces to create the front belt.) Cut the skirt and belt pieces on the fold.

3 **Assemble the bodice.** Lay the two bodice pieces on your work surface, right side up. Overlap the center fronts 1½ inches. Twist each piece at the shoulder, and then overlap the center backs 1½ inches. Baste the two bodice pieces together at center front and center back.

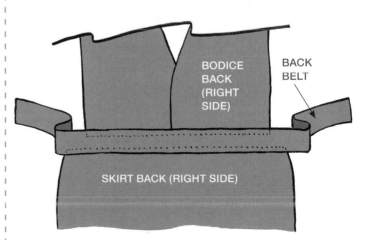

BODICE
BACK
(RIGHT
SIDE)

BACK
BELT

SKIRT BACK (RIGHT SIDE)

Center and sandwich the bodice and skirt between the two back belt pieces.

4 Assemble the back. Center the skirt's top edge between two belt pieces with their right sides in and raw edges aligned; sew through the three layers across the top of the skirt. Press the belt layers right side out. Fold under and press ½ inch to the wrong side along the top and bottom edges on each belt layer. Center and sandwich the bodice inside the two belt layers on the top edge. Then topstitch both long edges using a stretch straight stitch (looks like a lightning bolt). Leave both belt ends unsewn for now. Make sure not to fully erase your markings for the center front and the center back, as you will need them again later.

5 Finish the back belt. Customize the back belt to your size by cutting it to a width equal to your waist measurement plus 6 inches. Fold in the ends ¼ inch and edgestitch. Try on the dress by pulling it over your head, and overlap the belt ends at the center front as needed to fit. Hand-mark the overlap and hand-sew hooks and eyes to each belt end to secure them in place.

6 Finish the front belt. Assemble and finish the front. To create the front belt, sew the belt pieces in pairs, right sides together, on one short end. Center the strips on the skirt front as you did on the back and repeat the same application for the skirt and bodice. Try on the dress and customize the length of the belts to your size. Attach a belt buckle to the belt's right side. Turn under and edgestitch the left end to clean finish it. To wear, wrap the front belt around to crisscross in the back, and join the ends together in the front with the belt buckle.

Try on the dress, overlap the back belt at center front, and mark. Hand-sew hooks and eyes for a closure.

For sizes 2–10, use the red lines. For sizes 12–18, use the green lines.

Sizes 2–10: Bust 30 inches to 36 inches, waist 24 inches to 30 inches, hips 34 inches to 39 inches.

Sizes 12–18: Bust 37 inches to 43 inches, waist 31 inches to 37 inches, hips 40 inches to 45 inches.

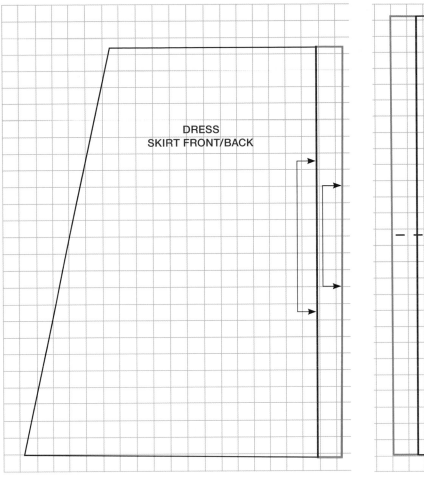

DRESS
SKIRT FRONT/BACK

DRESS
BODICE

SHOULDER

DRESS BELT

= 1 INCH BY 1 INCH

recycled-
sweater mittens

what you'll need

The Usual Suspects (see p. 121)
2 felted sweaters
½ yard Polarfleece
Template plastic or file folders
Patterns on pp. 134-135

Reinvent your winter woolens! Turn old wool sweaters—either your own or those you pick up from a secondhand store—into cute mittens lined with Polarfleece®. Men's sweaters, especially in size XL, are particularly great for this project: The bigger the sweater, the more mittens you can create.

Felt and deconstruct the sweaters

To felt the sweaters, run them through the washer and dryer. They will shrink and become thicker, and the knit stitches should become tighter or almost undefined. Wash and dry until the sweaters develop the texture you want.

1 Wash the sweaters. Machine-wash each sweater in the hottest water with detergent.

2 Dry on high. Dry the sweater on high/hot, periodically emptying the lint trap.

3 Continue to wash and dry. Repeat washing and drying the sweater until the texture is like felt.

4 Cut the sweaters apart on the seamlines. For ribbed sweaters, stretch and steam them as flat as possible.

Make the outside layers

When cutting the fabric for the mittens, there are a couple of things to remember: Don't forget to flip the pattern piece (found on p. 135) to accommodate for the right and left hands, and cut one layer at a time (the fabric is generally too thick to be cut precisely in double layers).

5 Prepare the mitten's back piece. Trace the mitten back pattern onto the fabric and cut it out.

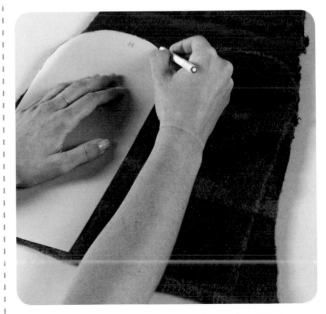

Trace the mitten back's pattern onto the sweater fabric.

6 Prepare the palm/lower thumb piece. **Trace the palm/lower thumb pattern onto the fabric and cut it out.**

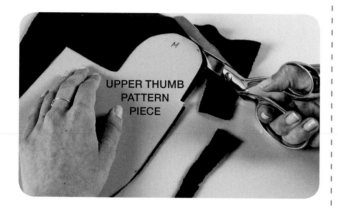

7 Prepare the upper thumb piece. **Trace the upper thumb pattern onto the contrasting sweater fabric and cut it out.**

8 Pin and sew the thumb. **With right sides together, pin the lower and upper thumb pieces together, around the thumb and across the palm. With a ⅜-inch-wide seam allowance, sew this seam, pivoting at the cut-out notch.**

9 Trim the mitten edges. **Trim the seam allowance to ¼ inch and then clip diagonally into the corner.**

Clip diagonally into the corner where you are pivoted.

10 Pin and sew the mitten. **Pin the thumb piece to the mitten back with right sides together and sew around the outer edge with a ⅜-inch-wide seam allowance. When you come to the thumb, fold it back and continue to stitch to the end, and then backstitch.**

Sew the mitten pieces together with a ⅜-inch seam allowance.

11 **Trim the seam allowance to ¼ inch. Repeat for the other mitten. Turn both mittens right side out.**

After sewing, trim the seam allowance.

Make the mitten lining

Soft Polarfleece lines the mittens. You can also add a label to the fleece on the inside of each pair.

12 Fold the Polarfleece in half. **Trace the three pattern pieces onto the Polarfleece and cut out the pieces.**

PALM/LOWER THUMB PATTERN

MITTEN BACK LINING

UPPER THUMB PATTERN

13 Add a label. **If you want to add a label, place it 3 inches from the wrist edge on the right side of one mitten back lining. Stitch it in place.**

Linda Teufel
PRIVATE COLLECTION

If you'd like to add a label, it's easiest to do so before sewing the lining pieces together.

14 Pin and sew the lining. **With right sides together, pin the lower and upper thumb pieces together. With a ½-inch-wide seam allowance, sew around the thumb and across the palm, pivoting at the cut-out piece.**

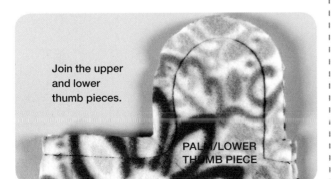

Join the upper and lower thumb pieces.

PALM/LOWER THUMB PIECE

15 Trim the palm/lower thumb edges. **Trim the seam allowance to ¼ inch, and then cut diagonally into the corner (see "Make the Outside Layers," step 9).**

16 Pin and sew the lining pieces. **Pin the thumb piece to the mitten back lining piece, right sides together, and sew around the curve, with a ½-inch-wide seam allowance. When you come to the thumb, fold it back and continue to stitch to the end and then backstitch.**

Sew around the lining pieces, and then backstitch at the cuff end.

17 Trim the sewn lining. **Trim the seam allowance to ¼ inch; repeat for the other mitten lining.**

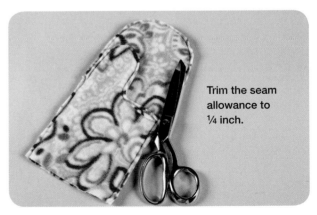

Trim the seam allowance to ¼ inch.

Join the layers

Insert the lining into the outer mitten and zigzag the cuff opening to finish.

18 Prep the lining. Place one lining on your hand, wrong side out.

19 Place the corresponding mitten over the lining. Pin the layers together, about 3 inches from the edge. Repeat with the other mitten.

20 Trim the cuff. To finish the wrist edge, trim ½ inch from the lining's edge, being careful not to cut the outer mitten.

21 Sew the cuff. Fold the outer layer inside ½ inch, pin in place, and then stitch with your machine's widest zigzag stitch and a stitch length of 1.5 mm. Be sure to catch the outer mitten, the lining, and the folded edge.

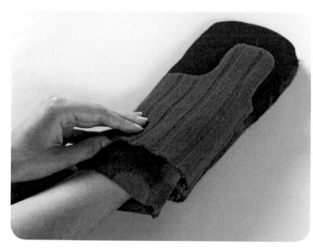

Slide the lining, wrong side out, into the mitten.

Pin the cuff, and then stitch a zigzag edge.

Children's mitten pattern

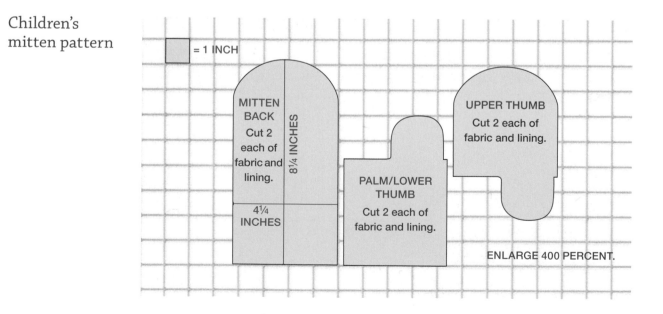

= 1 INCH

MITTEN BACK
Cut 2 each of fabric and lining.

8¼ INCHES

4¼ INCHES

PALM/LOWER THUMB
Cut 2 each of fabric and lining.

UPPER THUMB
Cut 2 each of fabric and lining.

ENLARGE 400 PERCENT.

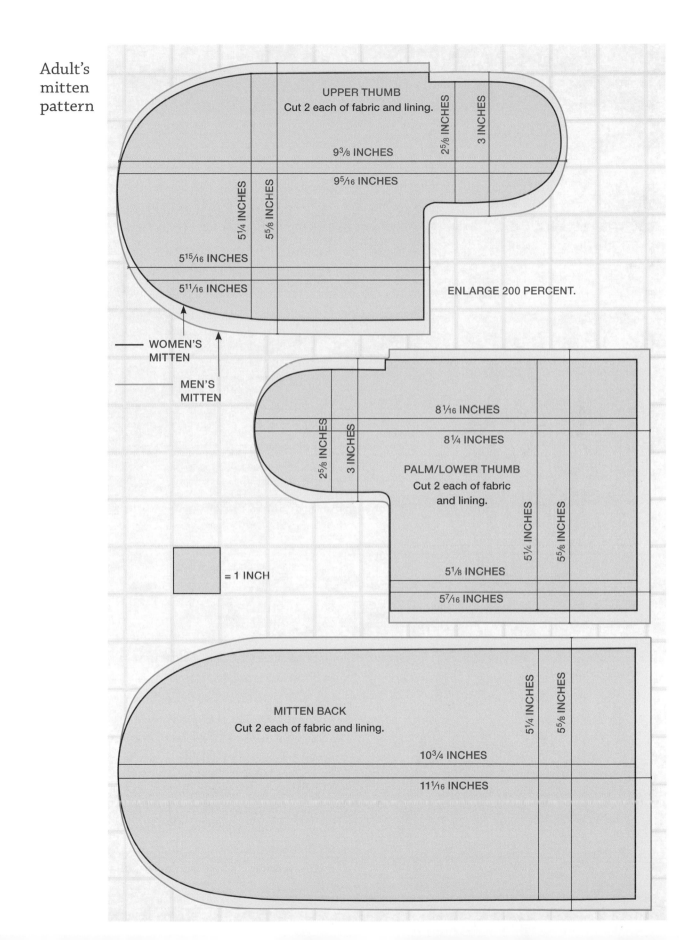

Adult's mitten pattern

UPPER THUMB
Cut 2 each of fabric and lining.

$2\frac{5}{8}$ INCHES
3 INCHES
$9\frac{3}{8}$ INCHES
$9\frac{5}{16}$ INCHES
$5\frac{1}{4}$ INCHES
$5\frac{5}{8}$ INCHES
$5\frac{15}{16}$ INCHES
$5\frac{11}{16}$ INCHES

ENLARGE 200 PERCENT.

——— WOMEN'S MITTEN

——— MEN'S MITTEN

$2\frac{5}{8}$ INCHES
3 INCHES
$8\frac{1}{16}$ INCHES
$8\frac{1}{4}$ INCHES

PALM/LOWER THUMB
Cut 2 each of fabric and lining.

$5\frac{1}{2}$ INCHES
$5\frac{5}{8}$ INCHES
$5\frac{1}{8}$ INCHES
$5\frac{7}{16}$ INCHES

= 1 INCH

MITTEN BACK
Cut 2 each of fabric and lining.

$5\frac{1}{4}$ INCHES
$5\frac{5}{8}$ INCHES
$10\frac{3}{4}$ INCHES
$11\frac{1}{16}$ INCHES

classic aprons

what you'll need

The Usual Suspects (see p. 121)

1 yard fabric

3 yards ribbon

Patterns on pp. 138–139

Sassy aprons are experiencing a revival as collectibles, chic kitchen gear, and fashion accessories. Sew up your own collection of fun, functional aprons inspired by the 1940s and 1950s. They're a great opportunity to play with fabric and stitching techniques, and you can make them, start to finish, in an hour or two. Have fun with prints: Quilt shops and home-decorating fabric stores are great sources for polka dots, large florals, conversation prints, and retro motifs. Cottons or cotton blends are a good choice; prewash them to soften. You can also use vintage kitchen towels and tablecloths. Cut away stains and worn spots, then piece as necessary for an apron with a unique retro style.

Flirty-Skirt Apron

This apron meets at the center back, so the pattern's top edge is one-sixth of your waist circumference. The length hits above the knee. Use self-fabric or ribbon for the waistband and ties. For the fabric waistband, cut a strip the length of the waist circumference and twice the desired width, plus seam allowances. The attached ties can be any length. With ribbon, cut a 3-yard length.

1 Seam. Use flat-fell seams (see the top photo on p. 139). Finish the top edges of the optional pockets. Baste them to the two side panels. Flat-fell all three panels together to encase the seam allowances. Trim one seam allowance to 1⁄8 inch. Press to one side. Fold the remaining seam allowance over it and topstitch.

2 Hem and edges. Turn up a double-fold hem (see the second from the top photo on p. 139). Finish the back edges with a narrow, double-fold edge. Then turn up a 1½-inch hem or sew a ruffle to the hem edge. Cut a length of

fabric twice as long as the apron's lower edge and 3 inches wide. Narrow-hem one edge and both short ends. Sew two lines of gathering stitches (long, loose, straight stitches). Pull the bobbin threads to gather, and pin the gathered strip to the apron. Sew and press the seam allowances toward the apron.

3 Waistband and ties. For a fabric waistband, cut two strips for the ties. Narrow-hem the long edges. Sew them to the waistband end, tucking to fit. Sew the band to the apron's top edge, right sides together. Fold the facing part of the band to the inside. Topstitch or hand-sew in place, catching the ties. For a ribbon waistband, fold the apron's top edge ½ inch to the right side. Cover the seam allowance with the ribbon. Topstitch along the top and bottom edge.

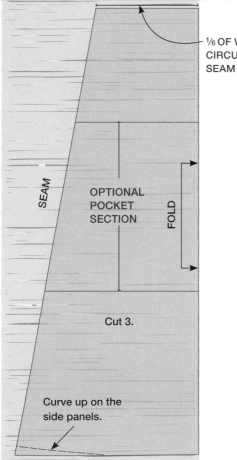

⅛ OF WAIST CIRCUMFERENCE SEAM

SEAM

OPTIONAL POCKET SECTION

FOLD

Cut 3.

Curve up on the side panels.

Bistro Apron

The steps are the same as the Flirty-Skirt Apron, but you skip the seam step and move directly to hem and edge. Use the width of the fabric as the apron's width, then trim as necessary to fit. The length falls below the knee. Make the waistband and ties long and skinny so they can wrap to the front. Add a variety of patch pockets. It's also easy to add a bib to this apron, as marked.

1 Hem and edges. Turn up a double-fold hem. Finish the back edges with a narrow,

double-fold edge. Then turn up a 1½-inch hem. Or sew a ruffle to the hem edge. Cut a length of fabric twice as long as the apron's lower edge and 3 inches wide. Narrow-hem one edge and both short ends. Sew two lines of gathering stitches on the remaining long edge. Pull the bobbin threads to gather and pin the gathered strip to the apron. Sew and press the seam allowances toward the apron.

2 Waistband and ties. For a fabric waistband, cut two strips for the ties. Narrow-hem the long edges. Sew them to the waistband end, tucking to fit. Sew the band to the apron's top edge, right sides together. Fold the facing part of the band to the inside. Topstitch or hand-sew in place, catching the ties. For a ribbon waistband, fold the apron's top edge ½ inch to the right side. Cover the seam allowance with the ribbon. Topstitch along the top and bottom edge.

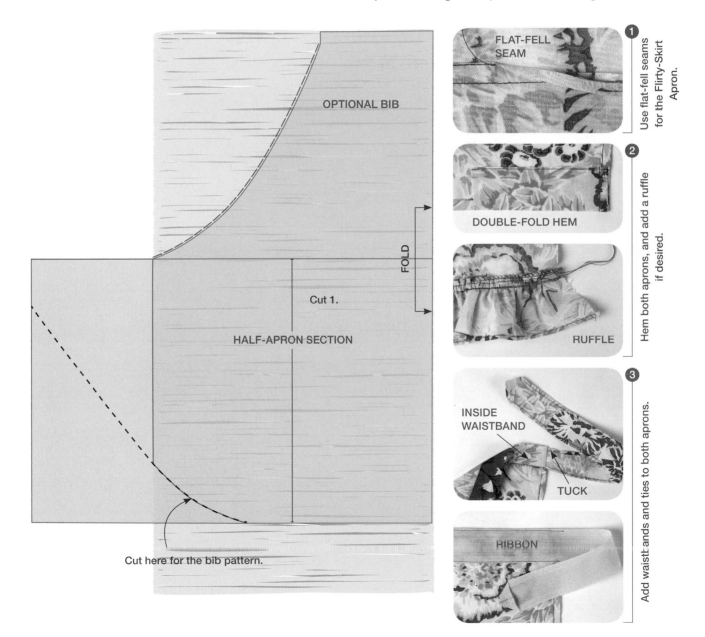

OPTIONAL BIB

FOLD

Cut 1.

HALF-APRON SECTION

Cut here for the bib pattern.

FLAT-FELL SEAM

1 Use flat-fell seams for the Flirty-Skirt Apron.

DOUBLE-FOLD HEM

RUFFLE

2 Hem both aprons, and add a ruffle if desired.

INSIDE WAISTBAND

TUCK

RIBBON

3 Add waistbands and ties to both aprons.

blanket coat

what you'll need

The Usual Suspects (see p. 121)

Fabric rectangle the width of your arm span and 1½ times the desired finished length of the jacket (if the fabric is narrower than your arm span, the jacket will have shorter sleeves; adjust the measurements accordingly)

Pattern on p. 142

You can make this easy-to-fit-and-sew jacket with an actual blanket or a blanketlike fabric, such as fluffy wool melton, soft felted wool, or even Polarfleece. The nice thing about starting with a blanket is the finished edges. If you're not using a blanket, choose a medium- to heavyweight material that doesn't ravel. The pattern, a basic bog coat, is very simple. The garment uses one rectangle of fabric, cut and folded to form the sleeves and body. For the trench coat look pictured, fashion a mock notched collar by adding an extra piece of fabric. You can belt the coat and add pockets, or keep it collarless and minimal.

Start with a rectangle

One piece of fabric, three cuts, and two seams are all you need. The shoulders and sleeves are formed by folding down the upper edge of the rectangle. The torso portion is made by wrapping the side edges toward center front. By adjusting the dimensions of the rectangle and the cuts, you can make many different looks.

1 Organize the measurements. **Unlike most garment sewing, the measurements for this jacket are broad. You want at least 10 inches of ease (see p. 104 for more) so you have plenty of wiggle room to wear the coat over sweaters and to match any patterns in the fabric. The arm depth is also the height of the armhole. Allow at least 10 inches for this coat so it can fit over other layers. Use your body measurements as a guide, but allow extra around the torso for ease.**

Give your folds a test run before you cut: Fold down the top edge of the fabric to check the length of the jacket. Then fold in the sides to the center. Eventually, you will cut horizontally along the edge that forms a sleeve.

2 Plan for pattern matching. **Before making any cuts, notice how the fabric's pattern matches where the cut edges meet: at the center front and horizontally across the chest. You want to fit your**

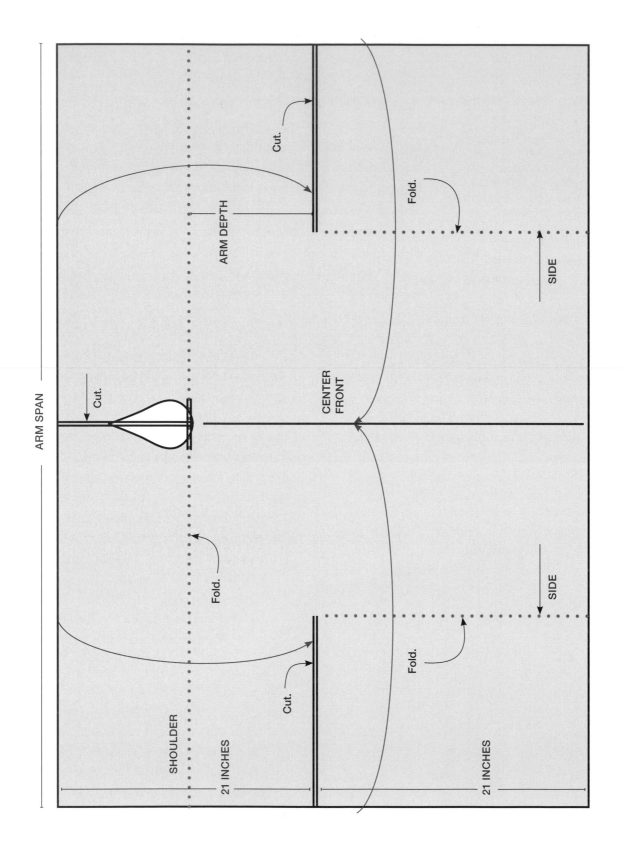

ARM SPAN

SHOULDER

21 INCHES

21 INCHES

ARM DEPTH

SIDE

SIDE

CENTER FRONT

Cut.

Cut.

Cut.

Fold.

Fold.

Fold.

body, but you also want any patterns to match (or at least to look planned). You can adjust the measurements to fit the fabric for a good-looking pattern match. With plaids, in particular, think before you cut. If a sleeve is too long, you can roll it up in a cuff. If a sleeve is too short, add a band of fabric at the hem, add a fur trim, or consider cutting the rectangle across the fabric's grain rather than with the grain. These are tricks you can use to match plaids attractively and make the fabric fit. When you are satisfied with the matching and you know you have adequate fabric to fold and wrap, make the three cuts for the jacket seams. The vertical cut at the center front should end at the shoulder fold. Then cut 3 inches on each side of the cut end horizontally across the fold, making the cut a T-shape. If you are adding the collar, use the T-shape to guide a curved cut around the neckline into a teardrop shape, as shown in the pattern diagram. Here, the center-front edges were overlapped to match the pattern, provide extra fabric for the lapel, and make the sleeves longer.

3 Cut a collar. For the collar, cut a strip that fits the neckline from the horizontal edge. Make it the width you want your lapel, then lap and sew it to the coat's neckline.

4 Organize the measurements. Lapped seams are the key to a smooth finish. First, attach the collar to the neckline with a lapped seam. Then, overlap and stitch the seams under the arm and across the front to form the jacket.

5 Finish the edges. The ideal edge is unfinished. That makes the project particularly easy. If you select a fabric that doesn't fray, you can leave the edge unfinished. But you can also sew a row or two of straight stitches about ½ inch from each unfinished edge to secure the weave. If you're working with an entire blanket that has finished edges, the only unfinished edges will be the center front and neck opening; on these you can add a binding or a facing or leave raw.

pajama pants

what you'll need

The Usual Suspects (see p. 121)

2 yards to 3 yards of soft 45-inch-wide woven fabric

1 yard of ¾-inch-wide grosgrain ribbon

½ yard of 1-inch-wide elastic

Safety pin

Scrap of fusible interfacing

Pattern on p. 147

Let's face it: Pajama pants are so comfortable that it's hard to change out of them. They're soft and cozy, and in most cases they just get better with age and multiple washings. Increasing your pajama wardrobe is fun and easy. First, determine your size according to the pattern. Next, choose a wonderful fabric, such as a flowy linen or an ultra-soft cotton shirting. Then follow our instructions to make your own can't-take-'em-off pants. Unless otherwise stated, use a ½-inch-wide seam allowance and finish the seam allowances by zigzagging or serging the raw edges together.

1 Choose a size. Select a size from the pattern (on p. 147) based on the hip (women) or waist (men) measurement.

2 Prep the fabric. Wash and dry your fabric as you will launder the finished garment. Press the fabric, cut it in half perpendicular to the selvage, and then place the layers right sides together, not folded, making sure the pattern is mirrored.

3 Sew the pant legs. With right sides together, align the inseams of one pant leg and sew. Repeat for the other leg.

4 Sew the crotch seam. Turn one leg right side out, and place it inside the other leg, with the raw edges of the crotch seam aligned and the inseams matched. Sew the crotch seam of the pants.

Align the edges of the crotch seam and sew.

Sew the inseam right sides together.

5 Hem the pants. Fold up and press the hem edge ¼ inch, then again ½ inch. Pin, then topstitch along the inner fold.

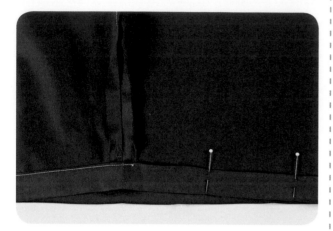

Pin, then topstitch the pant hems.

6 Make buttonholes in the casing area. Centered at the center front, fuse a 3-inch by 1-inch scrap of interfacing with its upper long edge parallel to and 1½ inches below the raw waist edge. Stitch a ¾-inch-long vertical buttonhole on each side of the center-front seam, with the buttonhole's top 1¾ inches from the waist edge. Cut the buttonholes open.

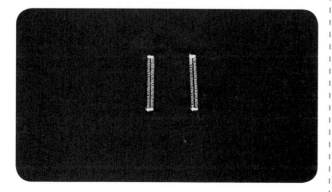

Sew the buttonholes in the waistband casing to hold the drawstring/elastic.

7 Sew the waistband casing. Fold down the waistband edge 1½ inches and press; press the raw edge under ¼ inch. Pin the casing in place, then topstitch along the inner fold.

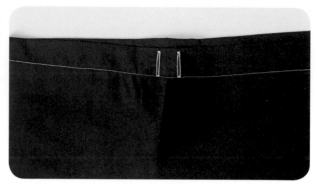

Pin, then topstitch the waistband casing.

8 Add the drawstring. Cut the grosgrain ribbon in half and sew a ribbon length to each end of the elastic. Attach a safety pin to one end of the strip end and, starting at one buttonhole, feed it through the waistband channel until the elastic is centered at the back of the pants. If desired, stitch in the ditch along the center-back seam to anchor the drawstring so it doesn't come out in the wash. Trim each ribbon end diagonally to minimize fraying.

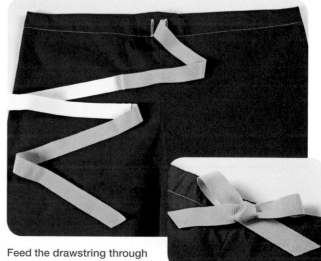

Feed the drawstring through the waistband.

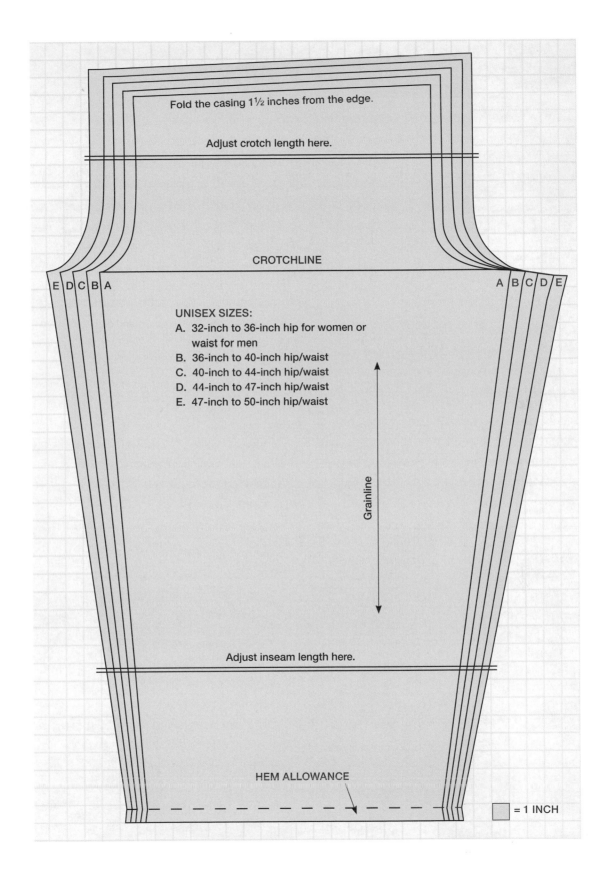

Fold the casing 1½ inches from the edge.

Adjust crotch length here.

CROTCHLINE

E D C B A   A B C D E

UNISEX SIZES:
A. 32-inch to 36-inch hip for women or
   waist for men
B. 36-inch to 40-inch hip/waist
C. 40-inch to 44-inch hip/waist
D. 44-inch to 47-inch hip/waist
E. 47-inch to 50-inch hip/waist

Grainline

Adjust inseam length here.

HEM ALLOWANCE

= 1 INCH

stylish wrap

what you'll need

The Usual Suspects (see p. 121)

About 1½ yards fabric

Paper, three pieces at least half your height in length

Grosgrain or silk ribbon (optional)

Gear up for cool weather with a cozy wrap. The nifty slit closure increases this wrap's cute and clever quotients. For this project, you'll make more than just the garment: You'll also create the pattern to fit your proportions, which will give you a perfect fit. Ask a friend to trace your shoulders. Then draft the pattern, choose your fabric, and sew the wrap. You can simply hem or bind the edges or create a luxuriously lined wrap.

Make the pattern

Start by standing with your hands on your hips in front of paper taped to the wall. Have a friend trace your neck, shoulders, and down your arms as described below.

1 Draft the back. Draw a curved line from 4 inches above one elbow to 4 inches above the other elbow, as shown on the facing page. Scoop out a back neckline from B to C and place the center back on the straight grain when you cut your fabric.

2 Draft two fronts. Use a yardstick to draw lines AE, BE, CF, and DG, as shown. Use the back pattern for reference. Mark the slit placement and grainlines as indicated.

3 Complete the pattern. Add ½-inch to ¾-inch hem allowances to the outer edges and ⅝-inch seam allowances to the shoulder seams.

Sew the wrap

The construction techniques required to make this wrap vary according to the fabric and desired style. Finish the slits last, so you're certain you like the placement.

4 Choose an edge. If you want to line the entire wrap with silky fabric, sew the shoulder seams first; then, with right sides together, join the layers around the outer edges and leave an opening for turning the wrap right side out. For a casual look, serge the seams and the edges instead. You could bind the edges with self fabric, grosgrain, or silk ribbon. Alternatively, fold the edges under, and topstitch, mitering the corner (creating a right angle) for a professional look, as shown.

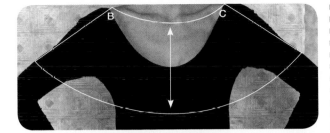

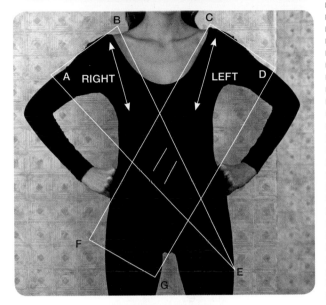

5 Mark the slits on both sides of your garment. Position a piece of bias fabric over the slash placement on the right side. With the wrong side up, stitch ⅛ inch away from the marked slit line.

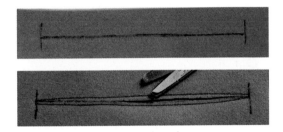

6 Cut through the two layers of fabric to create the opening. Then pull the bias facing through to the wrong side of the fabric, and press the edges.

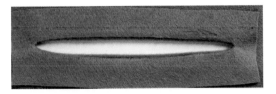

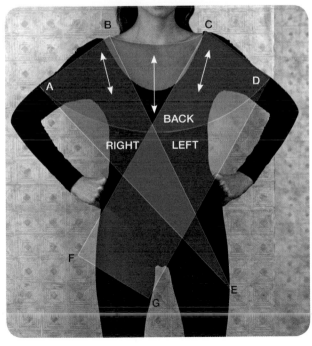

7 Topstitch around the opening to secure it. Then trim the edges of the bias facing.

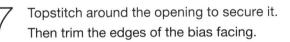

boxy tee

what you'll need

The Usual Suspects (see p. 121)

2 yards woven fabric

Pattern paper

This bold, boxy T-shirt is another project in which you make the pattern yourself. Once you've drafted it, the construction is so simple that you can whip up several in an assortment of fabrics—think luxe materials with body to accentuate the boxy shape. This top would look great in silk shantung, boiled wool, faux leather or Ultrasuede®, or even fabric embellished with beads or sequins.

Take measurements

Measure yourself in front of a mirror so you can see the tape measure while standing straight.

LENGTH (1). Hold the tape measure at your shoulder's highest point and let it drop straight down. Decide where you want the shirt hemline to sit on your body.

NECKLINE WIDTH AND DROP (2). For the neckline width, look in the mirror and hold the tape measure parallel to your shoulders in front of your neck and determine how wide you'd like the neckline to be. Next, without angling the tape, measure from your shoulder's highest point to where you want the front neckline drop to end. Note that you are not measuring a curve here— you do this when you draft the pattern.

BUST (3). Measure your bust and add 5 inches to 8 inches of ease. Add close to 5 inches if you don't want the tee to be too loose, and add closer to 8 inches if you want extra design ease.

SLEEVE/SHOULDER LENGTH (4). The sleeves are cut in one piece with the body. Determine where you'd like the sleeves to end, and measure from there to your center front at the neck.

SLEEVE WIDTH (5). To determine the sleeve width, measure around the fullest point of your biceps. Add at least 3 inches of ease.

HEM WIDTH (6). Measure around your body where you want the hem to be. Add the same ease as for the bust.

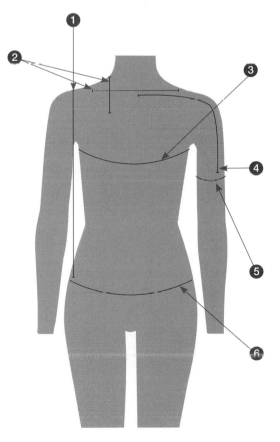

Convert measurements

Each pattern piece represents one-quarter of the body, so you need to divide some of the measurements by 4 or 2 to draft the pattern. Divide the bust, waist, and hip/hem circumferences by 4. Divide the neck width and sleeve opening by 2. These are the final numbers that you'll use for each measurement as you make the pattern.

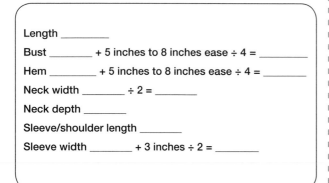

Length _____

Bust _____ + 5 inches to 8 inches ease ÷ 4 = _____

Hem _____ + 5 inches to 8 inches ease ÷ 4 = _____

Neck width _____ ÷ 2 = _____

Neck depth _____

Sleeve/shoulder length _____

Sleeve width _____ + 3 inches ÷ 2 = _____

Draft the pattern

The top's relaxed shape is easy to draft with just a few steps. Start with a large piece of pattern paper. Be sure to use the numbers calculated above and not your actual body measurements.

1 Mark the center front (CF), shoulder, and hemline. Straighten the pattern paper's left edge and label it *CF*. Measure and mark the shirt's length along the CF, leaving a few inches of pattern paper above and below. Next, draw two lines perpendicular to the CF, at the top and bottom of the line. Make the line at the top of the CF the shoulder/sleeve length. Make the line at the bottom of the CF the hem amount.

2 Draft the sleeve. From the end of the shoulder/sleeve line, draw a line parallel to the CF that equals the sleeve width amount. Next, draw a perpendicular line back toward the CF; this is the underarm seamline.

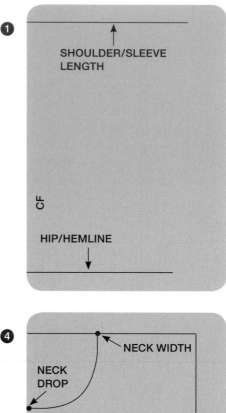

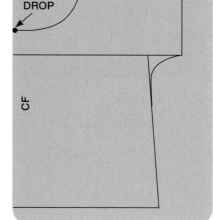

3 Create the side seams. Starting from the CF, mark the bust measurement along the underarm seamline. Connect this point down to the hip/hem point. Using a French curve or other curved ruler, blend the corner where the under-arm seam and the side seam meet into a gentle curve.

4 Draw the neckline. Starting from CF, mark the neck width along the shoulder/sleeve

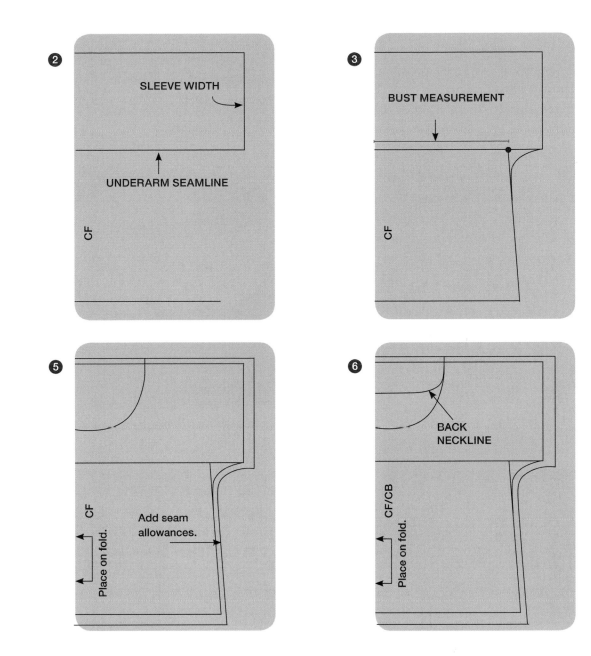

2 SLEEVE WIDTH → | UNDERARM SEAMLINE | CF

3 BUST MEASUREMENT ↓ | CF

5 CF | Place on fold. | Add seam allowances.

6 BACK NECKLINE | CF/CB | Place on fold.

line. Mark the neck drop along the CF, measuring down from the shoulder line. Join the two points with a smooth curve. Be sure the curve starts and finishes at a 90-degree angle.

5 Add ⅝-inch seam allowances to the shoulder and side seams. Add 1-inch hem allowances to the hem and sleeve openings. Do not add a seam allowance to the neckline. Write "Place on fold" on the CF line.

6 Make the back pattern. Cut out the front pattern and trace it onto another sheet of paper for the back pattern. The neckline is the only area that is different from the front. On the back pattern, raise the neck to about 2 inches from the shoulder line and redraw the neckline. Cut out the back pattern. Label the back piece and indicate the center back (CB). Write "Place on fold" on the CB line.

Sew the shirt

Once you've made the pattern, there are only a few steps left to construct the top. If you're making multiple tees, cut them all out at once, then sew them using an assembly-line approach.

7 Cut the shirt front and back. Place the pattern center front and center back along the fabric's folded edge. This creates two full garment pieces. Cut a 2-inch-wide bias strip equal to the neckline circumference plus 1 inch to finish the neckline edge later.

8 Sew the seams. With right sides together, sew the side seams using a straight stitch and finish them with a zigzag stitch or serging. (Note: Boiled wool generally does not ravel, so you don't have to finish it.) Sew the shoulder seams in the same way.

Sew and finish the seams.

9 Finish the neckline with a self-fabric bias tape. With right sides together, seam the bias strip's short ends together to form a loop. Fold and press under ½ inch on one long edge of the loop.

Create the neckline binding. Sew a bias strip in a loop, then press one long edge.

10 Sew the binding. Pin the right side of the bias tape's unfolded edge to the neckline's wrong side, distributing the bias tape evenly, and sew with a ½-inch seam allowance. Wrap the bias tape over the neckline edge to the right side, and pin with the folded edge just covering the first seam. From the right side, topstitch along the binding's folded edge.

Attach the neckline binding the garment.

11

Hem the sleeve openings and bottom hem. Use a ½-inch, double-fold, topstitched hem or a blind hem.

Sew the hems.

Finished hem (RS)

glossary of sewing terms

These common sewing terms are must-know info for savvy sewers.

ARMSCYE Armhole.

BACKSTITCH A strong hand-worked stitch that doubles back on the previous stitch.

BACK-TACK To sew a few stitches back and forth to anchor a seam's beginning or end.

BASTE To temporarily join fabric pieces with large, easily removable hand or machine stitches.

BIAS Any line diagonal to the crosswise and lengthwise grains. *True bias* is on a 45-degree angle to the selvage, which allows for the most stretch in wovens.

BIAS TAPE A fabric strip cut along the fabric's true bias; often used for binding. Also referred to as a *bias strip*.

BINDING A fabric strip used to cover or enclose raw edges.

BODKIN A small tool used for threading elastic, cording, etc., through a casing.

BOX PLEAT A pleat shaped from two knife pleats pointed away from each other.

CATCHSTITCH An X-shaped stitch used to join an edge flat to another fabric layer.

CENTER BACK (CB) The true vertical center on the garment's back.

CENTER FRONT (CF) The true vertical center on the garment's front.

CROSS-GRAIN The line perpendicular to the fabric selvage.

DART A folded and stitched fabric wedge that shapes a garment over curves. On a pattern, a dart point is marked by a dot. *Dart legs* are the lines that come to a stop at the pattern edge and indicate stitching.

DRAPE How a fabric hangs in a garment.

EASE 1. (n.) The difference between body measurements and garment measurements. Also defined as the amount of space in a garment that allows comfortable movement. 2. (v.) To slightly gather a longer fabric piece to fit a shorter one.

EDGESTITCHING Straight stitching sewn very close to the edge of a seam, trim, or outer edge; it prevents edges from stretching or rolling and supports the fabric.

FACING A partial lining used to finish exposed edges; at center front or back, neckline, armhole, or hem edges.

FEED DOGS These "teeth" move the fabric under the presser foot on the sewing machine. In the raised position, they "feed" the fabric. You can also drop the feed dogs to manually move the fabric freely in any direction.

FLAT-FELLED SEAM A seam in which all raw edges are encased by fabric and the allowances are sewn flat to the garment.

FRENCH CURVE A drafting tool for drawing smooth curves.

FUSIBLE WEB OR TAPE An adhesive product, sold in sheets or tape form, that glues two layers or fabric or trim together when heat is applied.

GATHER To draw up a length of fabric by pulling it into a series of puckers along a line of stitching.

GATHERING STITCH A long, loose, running or machine straight stitch that is pulled to create gathers.

GRAIN The thread orientation in woven fabric: lengthwise and crosswise. The lengthwise grain is parallel to the selvage and is the warp; cross-grain threads are perpendicular to the selvage and are the weft.

GRAINLINE Double-ended arrow symbol printed on a pattern, corresponding to the fabric's lengthwise grain.

GUIDE SHEET The set of cutting and sewing instructions that accompany a pattern.

HAND The way a fabric feels to the touch: smooth, crisp, etc.

HEM A garment's finished edge once the hem is sewn.

HYDROPHILIC FIBERS Fibers that absorb water.

HYDROPHOBIC FIBERS Fibers that repel water.

INSEAM The vertical seam that extends from the pant crotch to the hem.

INTERFACING Sew-in or fusible fabric used to stabilize fashion fabrics; it can also reinforce, add body, or shape a garment.

KNIFE PLEAT Consists of an outside fold that forms the pleat's visible edge, and an inside fold that is hidden behind the pleat. Knife pleats are usually in multiples, facing the same direction and continuing around a garment or repeating in small groups.

LINING A layer of fabric used to hide, protect, and beautify the interior of a garment or bag.

MITER To create a right angle corner between two strips of fabric by joining them with a seam that bisects the corner at a 45-degree angle.

MUSLIN Unbleached cotton fabric. Also a term used by designers to describe a test garment that checks fit and style.

NAPPED FABRIC A fabric whose surface fibers run in a specific direction, for example, velvet.

ON-GRAIN (LENGTHWISE GRAIN) The line parallel to the fabric's selvage, also called *grain*, *straight-of-grain*, and *warp threads*.

OVERLOCK STITCH SERGER Stitch in which you sew over the edge of one or two pieces of cloth for edging, hemming, or seaming.

PATTERN DRAFTING Drawing a paper pattern by positioning lines, points, and curves in a prescribed manner.

PICKSTITCH A variation on the backstitch where you backtrack only slightly and only a bead of thread is visible on the garment's right side.

PIN-FIT Fitting a garment by temporarily pinning in the seams, darts, or tucks to the right size.

PRESSER FOOT Sewing machine attachment that holds fabric to the feed dogs.

RAW EDGE Fabric's unfinished cut edge.

RIGHT SIDE (RS) The outside of a garment or the face side of fabric.

ROTARY CUTTER A circular cutting blade with a handle, used with a cutting mat.

SEAM Where two fabric pieces are sewn together. The *seamline* is the line that you sew along, typically ⅝ inch from the pattern piece's outermost edge.

SEAM ALLOWANCE (SA) The margin of fabric between the cutting line and the seamline. It is usually hidden inside the garment once the seam is sewn. In home sewing, the width is conventionally ⅝ inch, but it may be as narrow as ¼ inch or as wide as 1 inch.

SEAM FINISH Any technique that finishes a seam's raw edges.

SELVAGE The tightly woven edge that's parallel to the fabric's lengthwise grain.

SERGE To sew an edge or seam with a serger, or a machine that trims seam allowances and "overlocks" or wraps the fabric edge with thread.

SLEEVE CAP The sleeve section above the biceps line.

SLIPSTITCH A nearly invisible hand stitch used to join two folded edges or one folded edge to a flat surface. The thread travels inside the fold.

STABILIZER An underlayer used to support a fabric for machine embroidery or other embellishment technique.

STAYSTITCHING Machine stitches along a seamline that prevent the fabric from stretching before a seam is sewn.

STITCH LENGTH The length of a stitch established by the movement of the feed dogs.

STRAIGHT PINS Standard sewing pins, consisting of a straight piece of wire and a pointed end; used to secure fabric for cutting, sewing, and fitting.

STRAIGHT STITCH The most basic machine stitch, it produces a single row of straight, even stitches.

TACK To anchor two or more fabric layers together with a few hand or machine stitches.

TENSION The amount of pressure applied to a strand of thread by the tension disks of a sewing machine or serger. Adjust tension to accommodate threads and fabric of different weights.

TOPSTITCHING Decorative stitches sewn on a garment's right side.

UNDERLAP The lower fabric of two overlapped pieces of fabric.

WARP Lengthwise thread in woven fabric that runs parallel to selvage.

WEFT The crosswise threads in a woven fabric, from selvage to selvage.

WRONG SIDE (WS) Typically the inside of a garment or the back side of fabric.

YOKE A panel either across the shoulders or at the waistline from which the bulk of the garment hangs.

ZIGZAG A Z-shaped machine stitch, sometimes used to finish raw edges or to sew stretch seams.

ZIPPER FOOT A machine presser foot with a narrow toe, which enables you to stitch very close to the teeth of a zipper; also used to install piping and the like.

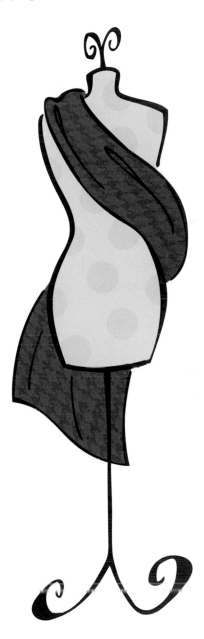

contributors

ROWENA ALDRIDGE is co-author of *Digital Flat Pattern: The Apparel Designer's Handbook* (Wild Ginger Software, 2009).

NANCY BENSIMON, a reader from Encinitas, California, provided the tip on p. 113.

LYNETTE RANNEY BLACK is the author of *Dream Sewing Spaces: Design & Organization for Spaces Large and Small* (Palmer/Pletsch Publishing, 2010).

SHARON BLAIR teaches sewing, patternmaking, and draping at Portland Sewing (portlandsewing .com) in Portland, Oregon.

CARRIE BLAYDES is co-author of *Fashion DIY: 30 Ways to Craft Your Own Style* (Sixth & Spring Books, 2007).

FRED BLOEBAUM was a contributing editor to *Threads* magazine.

BETTY BOLDEN, a reader from Bolton, Connecticut, provided the "Make it Simple" tip used on p. 35.

JAN BONES teaches patternmaking and garment design at the University of Manitoba in Canada.

CLAUDIA BUCHANAN is owner of Home Fashions U (HomeFashionsU.com) in Peoria, Arizona, which offers online sewing education and home décor sewing supplies.

RUTH CIEMNOCZOLOWSKI is a designer and stylist for motion pictures in Omaha, Nebraska.

SANDRA ERICSON is the director of the Center for Pattern Design (CenterforPatternDesign.org) and has been teaching pattern design for more than 30 years.

CAROL FRESIA is a *Threads* technical editor and sews and writes in Chicago, Illinois.

GAY GERLACK sews, designs, and writes in Martinez, California.

JACQUE GOLDSMITH teaches home sewers and industry professionals in Seattle, Washington.

PAMELA HOWARD teaches sewing in Atlanta, Georgia.

JENNIFER JAMAL is the former education director at Haberman Fabrics and an avid sewer.

PATRICIA KEAY creates couture dresses in her Massachusetts home.

SUSAN KHALJE is a contributing editor to *Threads* magazine and an author and teacher who specializes in couture sewing techniques.

LINDA LEE owns The Sewing Workshop pattern line (SewingWorkshop.com) and designs, teaches, and writes about sewing techniques and garment design.

ANNA MAZUR served as president of American Sewing Guild and sews and writes in Avon, Connecticut.

SARAH MCFARLAND is associate editor at *Threads* magazine.

SUSIE NELSON is a custom clothier and instructor in Oakland, Nebraska.

JUDITH NEUKAM is senior technical editor at *Threads* magazine and writes and hosts the *Teach Yourself to Sew* video series.

ANNIE O'CONNOR is a former assistant editor at *Threads* magazine.

SARAH OPDAHL is a special projects editor for The Taunton Press.

CAL PATCH (HodgepodgeFarm.net) is an author, designer, and teacher.

LORRAINE PRATT, a reader from Layton, Utah, provided the "Make it Simple" tip used on p. 7.

MARY RAY is a contributing editor to *Threads* magazine.

PHYLLIS RETTKE, a reader from Bellevue, Washington, provided the "Make it Simple" tip on p. 111.

LINDA ROCK, a reader from Winnipeg, Manitoba, Canada, provided the "Make It Simple" tip used on p. 101.

MARY ROEHR (www.maryroehr.com) is the author of six books and a DVD on sewing.

JENNIFER SAUER is a former senior editor at *Threads* magazine.

JENNIFER STERN teaches and writes about sewing and is the creator of J Stern Design Patterns (jsterndesigns.com).

LINDA TEUFEL is the founder of the Dragon Threads publishing firm (DragonThreads.com).

ELISE WILLIAMS, a reader from Frankford, Ontario, Canada, provided the "Make it Simple' tip used on p. 18.

CHRIS WOJDAK, a reader from La Mesa, California, provided the "Make it Simple" tip used on p. 13.

FIONN ZARUBICA is a managing partner of CostumeAndTextileCollectionCare.com in Los Angeles, California.

resources

Events and Organizations

AmericanSewingExpo.com

ASG.org

Craftandhobby.org

Creativfestival.ca

MakerFaire.com

NationalSewingCouncil.org

Quilts.com

SewExpo.com

SewGreen.org

SewingExpo.com

Sewing.org

SewingProfessionals.org

Vintage Equipment and Patterns

Creativebug.com

DecadesofStyle.com

Ebay.com

Etsy.com

EvaDress.com

SoVintagePatterns.com

Vpll.org

Classes

FabricLand.com

HabermanFabrics.com

JoAnn.com

Sewing.org

Sewing.PatternReview.com

TeachYourselfToSew.com

ThreadsMagazine.com

Craftsy.com

Setting Up Your Sewing Space

ERGONOMIC FURNITURE AND TOOLS

Dritz.com

ErgoGenesis.com

ErgonomicAdvantage.com

PainFreeQuilting.com

TOOLS AND SUPPLIES

AccuQuilt.com

ACMoore.com

AllBrands.com

Amazon.com

ArtStuff.net

Beverlys.com

Bonanza.com

BSewInn.com

Clover-USA.com

Cochenille.com

DiscountSchoolSupply.com

ENasco.com

FabricsAndButtons.com

Gingher.com

HancockFabrics.com

JoAnn.com

KaiScissors.com

NancysNotions.com

PGMDressForm.com

QualitySewing.com

SewingEmporium.com

SewingPlanet.com

Sew-Materialistic.com

SpinBlessing.com

Stuff4Sewing.com

ThermoWebOnline.com

Wardrobesupplies.com

WAWAK.com

WidgetSupply.com

SEWING MACHINES AND SERGERS

Babylock.com

Bernina.com

Brother-USA.com

HusqvarnaViking.com

Janome.com

Jukihome.com

PfaffUSA.com

SingerCo.com

FABRICS

Threadsmagazine.com (for a list of online fabric retailers)

THREADS

JoAnn.com

MoodFabrics.com

Working with Patterns

BurdaStyle.com

McCall.com

Simplicity.com

INDEPENDENT PATTERNS

patterncompanies.com.

Threadsmagazine.com (for a comprehensive list)

Dress Forms

PROFESSIONAL

PGMDressform.com

Ronis.com

SuperiorModel.com

VMRForms.com

WolfForm.com

CUSTOMIZABLE

FabulousFit.com

MyTwinDressforms.com

DIAL ADJUST

Dritz.com

CUSTOM-MADE

DressFormDesigning.com

MyTwinDressforms.com

SewingLingerie.com

Project Resources

SILK SCARF

DharmaTrading.com

JRBSilks.com

Orientalsilk.com

PrintedSilkFabrics.com

RedRockThreads.com

SuperiorThreads.com

ThaiSilks.com

GRECIAN TANK

MoodFabrics.com

Simplicity.com

WRAP DRESS

JoAnn.com

FLOOR CUSHION

Shop.HomeFashionsU.com

UpholsterySuppliesAndFoam.com

CLASSIC APRON PATTERNS

Ebay.com

Oldpatterns.com

SoVintagePatterns.com

TheBlueGardenia.com

metric equivalents

One inch equals approximately 2.54 cm. To convert inches to centimeters, multiply the figure in inches by 2.54 and round off to the nearest half centimeter, or use the chart below, whose figures are rounded off (1 cm equals 10 mm).

⅛ in. = 3 mm	9 in. = 23 cm
¼ in. = 6 mm	10 in. = 25.5 cm
⅜ in. = 1 cm	12 in. = 30.5 cm
½ in. = 1.3 cm	14 in. = 35.5 cm
⅝ in. = 1.5 cm	15 in. = 38 cm
¾ in. = 2 cm	16 in. = 40.5 cm
⅞ in. = 2.2 cm	18 in. = 45.5 cm
1 in. = 2.5 cm	20 in. = 51 cm
2 in. = 5 cm	21 in. = 53.5 cm
3 in. = 7.5 cm	22 in. = 56 cm
4 in. = 10 cm	24 in. = 61 cm
5 in. = 12.5 cm	25 in. = 63.5 cm
6 in. = 15 cm	36 in. = 92 cm
7 in. = 18 cm	45 in. = 114.5 cm
8 in. = 20.5 cm	60 in. = 152 cm

photographer & illustrator credits

GLEE BARRE
Page 62 (bottom)

ROSANN BERRY
Pages 32, 77, 78 ,82 (top), 99, 104,
124 (top)

EMILY BRONSON
Pages 88, 123, 142, 147

JAMEY CHRISTOPH
Pages 85, 106, 107

JACK DEUTSCH
Pages 76, 83, 84, 122, 125 (top right), 126, 128, 148, 149 (left)

CHRISTINE ERIKSON
Pages 24, 25 (center), 37, 38, 39, 40, 41, 115

SLOAN HOWARD
Pages 7, 8, 10, 11, 12, 13, 15, 16, 17, 29, 34, 35, 43, 44, 45, 46, 47, 49, 50, 51, 52, 53, 54, 55, 62 (top), 63, 67, 68, 69, 70, 71, 72, 73, 77, 79, 80, 81, 82 (bottom), 89, 90, 91, 103, 123 (bottom), 124 (bottom), 125 (left top, left center, left right, bottom right), 130, 131, 132, 133, 134, 140, 141, 143, 144, 145, 146, 149 (right), 150, 154, 155

BOB LA POINTE
Page 68

GLORIA MELFII
Pages 77, 134

CASEY LUKATZ
Pages 4, 7 (bottom), 22, 23, 26, 30, 36, 42, 57, 61, 64, 92, 100, 112, 120, 159

MELANIE MENCARELLI
Pages 95, 96, 97

KAREN MEYER
Page 25 (right)

SCOTT PHILLIPS
Pages 9, 14, 18, 19, 21, 66, 74, 75, 86, 87, 108, 109, 110, 111, 136, 137, 138 (right), 139 (right)

KAT RIEHLE
Pages 151-153

CAROL RUZICKA
Pages 117, 118, 119

COURTESY OF SIMPLICITY
Pages 94, 101, 102

NICOLE SMITH
Pages 127, 129

LISA SUMMERELL
Pages 138 (left), 139 (left)

index

If you like this book, you'll love everything about *Threads*.